Praise for *Dancing in the Dash*

"With special resonance for this mon_____ _____ country's history, Lauri, a friend of many ye___, shares a creative and compelling portrait of a Black woman making
her mark, while handling her personal and professional
lives with grace. Her story is a compelling testament to
the transcendence of resolve, perseverance and resilience across generations of an American family."

—Ambassador Susan E. Rice,
former US national security advisor

"From private dinners with revolutionaries and heads
of state to marathon strategy sessions with presidents
and diplomats, Lauri Fitz-Pegado walks gracefully as
a citizen of the world. Bolstered by a childhood of love
and privilege, her personal quest for excellence created
a launching pad for a life of purpose, impact, and adventure. At moments of inevitable grief and heartache,
she drew sustenance from deeply cultivated friendships and her early training as a dancer. *Dancing in the
Dash* will challenge us all to do more and will inspire
young women to dream and dare to make a difference."

—A'Lelia Bundles,
author of *On Her Own Ground:
The Life and Times of Madam C. J. Walker*

"Lauri Fitz-Pegado shares her captivating life story with
an honesty, insightfulness, and humanity that makes
her book inspired and inspiring. Truly a 'page-turner'
from start to finish."

—Mavis Staines,
artistic director and CEO, Canada's National Ballet School

"Lauri-Fitz-Pegado's *Dancing in the Dash* provides an interesting peek inside the development of a performing artist in a challenging time."

—Virginia Johnson,
artistic director, Dance Theatre of Harlem

"Secretary Ron Brown was a singularly impressive figure, and in his time at the Commerce Department gathered the most remarkable, enthusiastic, and diverse group of young colleagues I ever had the pleasure of meeting in my time as ambassador. Lauri was not just a part, but a key formal and informal leader of this group. I am so pleased that she has decided to present this collection of moments and memories from her life and career, not only because it is a record of history but because it is a hugely enjoyable work of literature. I hope that through the book she will continue to inspire, entertain, and teach, as she has done all her life."

—Dr. Miomir Zuzul,
founder of Dubrovnik International University,
former ambassador of Croatia
to the United Nations and the United States,
and former minister of foreign affairs of Croatia

"Lauri and I met through our mutual time in the private sector and soon discovered our shared views on diversity and inclusion. I was unaware, however, how complex and fascinating her life and career had been until I read this brilliantly written memoir. At this moment when racism is at the center of debate and discussion in the US, her life story provides valuable insights not often addressed or understood."

—Peter Woicke,
a former managing director of the World Bank
and CEO of the International Finance Corporation

"A book full of life and memories, written with spontaneity and elegance, which casts an exciting light on the world of US politics and foreign affairs over the past thirty years. Lauri remains a model for minority women who are determined to achieve their dreams, despite all kinds of gender and race prejudices. She is talented, serious, and committed. And more than that, she is a great friend."

—Jean-Robert Estimé,
former foreign minister of Haiti

"Lauri Fitz-Pegado spent a very successful professional life solving hard problems for sophisticated institutions and leaders who never imagined the rich personal history and life she carried with her. Thank God she is now sharing with us the motivations, passions, and fears which make her luminous. It's a great read and a fascinating story."

—Robert Raben,
founder and president, The Raben Group

Dancing
in the
Dash

Bold Story Press, Washington, DC 20016
www.boldstorypress.com

This book is a memoir, and it reflects the author's present
recollections of experiences over time.

First edition published September 2021

Library of Congress Control Number: 2021911153

ISBN: 978-1-954805-15-6 (hardcover)
ISBN: 978-1-954805-04-0 (paperback)
ISBN: 978-1-954805-05-7 (e-book)

Text and cover design by Laurie Entringer
Cover photo, author photo, and photo editing by Edward C. Jones

Photos are from the author's personal collection unless
otherwise noted. Sheet music that appears on pages 204,
208, 214, 216, and 221 is courtesy of Public Domain Company.

10 9 8 7 6 5 4 3 2 1

Dancing
in the
Dash

My Story of Empowerment,
Diplomacy, and Resilience

LAURI J. FITZ-PEGADO

**BOLD
STORY
PRESS**

Washington, DC

For my mother Joyce Mayes Fitz
1930–2014

". . . Is there—is there balm in Gilead?
—tell me—tell me, I implore!"
EDGAR ALLEN POE, "THE RAVEN"

Balance is a critical requirement for success in life and in ballet. A six-foot-tall sculpture dominates a special place in my home—"Eclipse" is a tall, bronze sculpture of a dancer perched atop a large ball. The muscular body is molded into a stylized arabesque: the demi-point of the supporting leg balancing on the globe. The three-foot tall bronze sculpture is mounted on a three-foot tall rotating marble base. The late African American artist Tina Allen created this defining and imposing work. It serves as a constant reminder to me of graceful power, and of the strength, delicate precision, and tenuousness of balance.

"Life is the dancer and you are the dance."
ECKART TOLLE

*"When you dance you can enjoy the
luxury of being you."*
PAULO COELHO

*"rise up fallen fighters / unfetter the stars /
dance with the universe & make it ours"*
NTOZAKE SHANGE

Contents

Foreword

But what of Black women? . . . I most sincerely doubt
if any other race of women could have
brought its fineness up through so devilish a fire."
—W. E. B. DU BOIS

W. E. B. Du Bois, with his full discernment about the plight of Black women, posited, "But what of Black women? I most sincerely doubt if any other race of women could have brought its fineness up through so devilish a fire." Indeed, for Black girls and women, coming of age and growing old in America, life here can be a devilish fire. Picture a young Black girl growing up at any time in the history of this country, and you will imagine a life complicated by limits to her opportunities, with difficult hurdles placed in her path that she must overcome, although without a clear sense that she will overcome. That devilish fire begins at birth, if she and her mother survive her birth, and continues through countless affronts, furies, and indignities, until hopefully, prayerfully, we find her standing straight and tall, having risen through it all, and arrived joyful and intact in all her adult fineness. Du Bois. Period. We marvel that in so few words, he captures the very essence of the life of a Black woman in America.

In many ways, Lauri is the Black woman who came up in the midst of that devilish fire. She saw its smoldering flames through the back window of her father's car after areas of DC bore the brunt of Black people's anger and frustration following the assassination of Dr. Martin Luther King, Jr.; she felt its uncomfortable warmth while holding tight to the hand of her father, as the white robed and hooded Klansmen marched by on Main Street in Warrenton, North Carolina; she and her Black friends felt the flicker of its flame as it teased at the preteen girls who sat in the balcony of the movie theater, separated by law and custom, from the white children who occupied the main auditorium below; she experienced it as a girl in high school when she laughed to cover the pain of embarrassment after white schoolmates termed her natural hair as seemingly shocked by an electrical current.

Yet, in so many ways, Lauri's life does not exemplify that of a typical Black girl in that she has overcome structural and institutional limitations by dint of discipline, parental direction, blessings from on high, and sheer willpower, to propel her over hurdles placed in her path. She has met and shared space with some of the greatest icons of our time, from Mozambique's Samora Machel to Tanzania's Julius Nyerere to Namibia's Sam Nujoma to President Bill Clinton. She once spent an afternoon with the fearsome leader of Panama, El Jefe General Omar Torrijos, who thankfully never guessed at her American citizenship; and was in the room for meetings with Rabin, Arafat, and King Hussein as part of delegations accompanying Commerce Secretary Ron Brown. But, as charmed as Lauri's life has been, it has not been without pain. The loss of her dear friend and mentor, Ron Brown, whose tragic death in an airplane crash in Croatia broke the hearts of so many, including his close friend, President Bill Clinton, is chronicled here in cathartic detail. Lauri writes of moments of strength and vulnerability, historic and everyday moments, as she weaves her way through a magnificent series of life experiences. Lauri's life has been, and is, both limitless and privileged; she exemplifies a life unbounded and with unfettered opportunities. And through it all,

Lauri has worked, prayed, laughed, cried, and loved, and always, she has danced. Because, throughout it all, there was ballet. Ballet figures prominently in Lauri's life, from classes she attended in her early childhood in New York, to studying classical ballet in an iconic school in DC owned by two incredible Black women, to being welcomed into a ballet company in Santo Domingo while she was posted at the U.S. Embassy in the Dominican Republic, to classes in major cities across the globe where her travels took her. Like a sweet godparent, always there cheering her on, and waiting in the wings to catch her when she fell, ballet has enveloped her with love and welcome, provided discipline as it helped raise her up, and saved her many a time. Dance has been an important loom weaving joy, pain, love, and celebration into the tapestry of Lauri's story.

First and foremost, however, is the place that family holds in Lauri's heart and in the pages of her memoir. Theirs is a quintessential American family, with roots deep in the soil of rural North Carolina, in Washington, DC, and in the bustling towns of the Maryland suburbs. And just as American is the Fitz and Mayes families' extended family trees with branches reaching into the white, Native American, and African Americans communities. The stories Lauri shares capture intimate and sweet moments, like the bus rides with her brother to her grandparents' home in Warrenton. They paint a portrait of a time gone by where Lauri learned to make barbeque sandwiches for customers at the Fitz Grocery store owned by her grandparents. We are drawn into the joy of fun times in the shadow of the nation's capital on the 4th of July, and the curiosity of watching a treasured uncle, who passed for white, attempt to come up with an explanation about the origins of his darker-skinned niece.

Historically, there are few memoires written by Black women chronicling their lives in this the greatest nation on earth. There was little record made of our joys and struggles, our accomplishments and failures, our strengths and vulnerabilities, the celebrations and bitter betrayals, the healing and trauma, the births and burials. The writer of a memoir gives herself the opportunity to remember, and in remembering, gives honor to all her many stages and selves. From the little girl whose mother and father leave her for academe in Europe to the woman who leaves a husband of 15 years, each girl is Lauri, and each one is celebrated in this book.

I've known Lauri since the late '70s when I met her the year I entered Vassar. I had flown eight thousand miles from an idyllic girlhood in East Africa, and during my first week at Vassar, met a senior who exuded sophistication and savoir faire. We were on campus only one year together, but I knew from the first that I would seek out her friendship long into the future. So, as time has moved on, and our college years slip far back in the rearview mirror, my first meeting with Lauri still remains an unspoiled memory I periodically unwrap like a gift, and give thanks to the fates that blessed me with a dear friend, as I pined for the childhood I left behind in the Rift Valley, and adjusted to a new life in the Hudson Valley.

Lauri's memoir speaks much of such long and precious bonds, with over five decades of friends scattered across its pages, each encounter more special and fascinating than the last. Lauri describes her friends and friendships in ways lyrical and beautiful. She takes us wading through a sea of giant sunflowers in Santibáñez; we share the excitement of traveling from Madrid to Milan in the cattle car of a train on the way for a visit with her boyfriend's aunt, a noted soprano, and her husband, a Czech-born baron; and we share her awe at meeting a Black sculptor and graphic artist in a restaurant covered in flowers and named for the Mexican birthday song. Lauri holds her friends close, and across a time continuum that doesn't end. With Lauri, you know the bond of friendship will only become tighter as the years go by.

This memoir is a love letter about family and friendship; about love and loss; and, about the work needed to keep your sanity when things around you fall apart. At times, it can be easy to push aside our history, to bury the past in small, neat packages, put away and forgotten like ancient history. We file away our memories, joyful and painful, and seldom bring them out to scrutinize and assess. There are reasons for this, some driven by unaddressed anxiety, and some by our need to protect the little bits of joy that appear like the spring flowers on the bushes around our homes. Sometimes, however, in burying those tiny packages, we inadvertently drop one like a seed into soil, and give it a moist place to grow. We've pressed the soil firmly, hoping, as we bury it, we ensure it never again sees the light of day. While hoping to leave that thing in the past, we've actually placed it into fertile soil from which a growing vine peeks out and demands notice. Memoirs give us the opportunity to give our memories their due; to unpack and sort through the good and the ugly, the sweet and the savory. In doing so, maybe we come to terms with it all, and find acceptance. So, to paraphrase Dr. Du Bois, what of this Black woman? What of this woman, reaching the age of majority in a country that is still coming to terms with accepting her; where the image of the winner is white and male, how did she overcome and achieve unbelievable success in public sector positions in the Foreign Service, at the Department of Commerce and in the private sector, in public relations and lobbying positions representing people and nations? All while living Black and female? Lauri's memoir gives us a window into how she navigated the structural constraints imposed by a system constructed to limit her. Lauri's experiences and personal perspectives are timely, especially as the country grapples with its racial history. So, thank you, Dr. Du Bois, for your belief and confidence in Black women—despite the devilish fire set out to consume her, this particular Black woman has brought up her fineness and still she stands.

Karen Leslie Cox
Washington, District of Columbia

CHAPTER ONE

Curtain First, Then Lights

The bright southern sunlight blazed through the window of the back room of the house where I slept when I awakened to feel a warm body next to me. When my parents returned to Warrenton, North Carolina, where I was living with my paternal grandparents, it seemed an eternity had passed. I was only three years old, and Mom must have crawled quietly into bed with me right after they arrived at the house late the previous night. The next morning, my big round eyes, which then occupied half of my face, met her smile, and I said resolutely, "You are not my Mommy. My Mommy leaves lipstick on the pillow." My mother's makeup regimen was just enough with lipstick and maybe a quick swipe of face powder. She usually failed to remove every trace of the orangey-colored lipstick she liked to wear (she never used any shade of pink or red lip color). When she washed her face before bed and applied white creamy Noxzema on her velvety skin, her lips always left a trace of orange on her pillow.

Being separated from my father for two years and from my mother for almost a year at such an early age must have contributed to my becoming a child beyond her years; I was independent and opinionated, precocious and obedient. I now understand why from the time I was very young, I spoke and carried myself like a diminutive old woman; I was born an old soul.

Both of my parents, my mother Joyce Mayes Fitz and my father Norman Alonzo Fitz, came from small towns and families of limited means but dared to travel to Europe as a first foreign adventure; not as tourists, but to live. My father had applied to the very few medical schools in the US available to aspiring colored doctors but was not lucky enough to gain admission. In a fortuitous move, a fellow Howard University graduate, Bart Vance, had discovered a medical school in Switzerland that accepted him, and he had encouraged Dad to follow his path to Europe. In a strange twist of fate, Bart's former wife, Yvonne De Vastey, and Dad have created a life together since my mother's death in 2014.

Dad attended medical school for a year in Switzerland and for another one in Germany. He never completed his medical studies, but instead returned to the US with Mom, who had joined him in Germany during his second year, and who was then pregnant with my brother Bruce. Moving to Europe was a bold move for a married

Lauri at maternal grandparents' home, circa 1958

Mom with Lauri, circa 1957

Dad, circa 1954   Mom, circa 1954

colored man with a young child in the 1950s. During his first year away in Switzerland in 1957, my mother and I stayed behind with her parents and youngest sister, Connie, in her childhood home in Brentwood, Maryland. His second year, my mother joined him in Mainz, Germany. She described to me how she felt cold all the time and was watched constantly by curious Germans. She remembered their stares being more fascinated than menacing. When they were in a restaurant, she felt and saw eyes following her fork from plate to mouth. Neither she nor my father spoke German, so she was lonely and found the constant scrutiny intrusive and unsettling, whether well intentioned, merely curious, or something else. Her theory about the extreme attention was that the Germans had seen darker-skinned Africans who lived in their country in small numbers but were unfamiliar with much lighter-skinned Black Americans. She omitted what I surmised was a contributing factor—my parents were an extremely attractive couple. I always thought my mother at that age resembled the Italian actress Sophia Loren, and my father was also quite easy on the eyes, which I'm sure contributed to his popularity in college and in Switzerland where he became a ping-pong champion. Mom openly expressed her half-playful and half-judgmental consternation about how he simultaneously managed his rigorous studies and his successful sports pursuits, while she raised me alone in the early years of her teaching career, living back home at her parents' house. Perhaps joining her husband in Mainz during his second year was to satisfy her own curiosity. They returned to the US when Mom became pregnant with my brother Bruce in Germany. Dad never finished medical school.

Back in the US in 1959, Dad began working at laboratories, and his uniform was a white lab coat that I associated with Dr. Kildaire, the television character. In the evenings, in our neighborhood, the older women sitting on their front porches to catch the summer breeze looked at him with prideful smiles as his athletic stride and powerful gait brought him home in that white jacket which further illuminated his suntanned skin.

I spent many days perched on Grandma Mayes' front porch so I would be the first to spot him approaching as he returned from work. The colorful sunsuits I wore ended where my bare little legs hung over the top porch step. My hair was neatly combed, brushed, and parted into three sections with matching hair ties clasping my dangling twists. One day, the second I saw my dad coming up the walk, I proclaimed in my outside voice for all within earshot, "Norman's home." Grandma Mayes, also sitting in her favorite chair nearby, corrected me, saying, "You mean your Daddy's home." I retorted haughtily, "Him name Norman, ain't him." Everyone burst out laughing, and from that moment on those words became part of family lore. Just a few years ago, my father gave me a silver charm bracelet with a heart inscribed with that very phrase. I imagine that my mother, an English teacher, must have cringed at my poor grammar even as she joined in the laughter.

4

I became an adult intent on exceeding expectations; some expectations that I perceived, and many others that were self-imposed. My dad was strict, demanding, and critical, pushing us to always do better. His booming bass voice was frightening enough without him lowering it an octave when he really meant business.

From those early days in Brentwood and in Warrenton, my life became a series of sprints to cross a finish line that kept reemerging farther down the road. Upon seeing the finish line a few strides away, I found myself digging deep for that second wind to tackle the next one without stopping to catch my breath. I worked equally hard to prepare myself for the preliminary heats, striving to finish first in the qualifying rounds. My guiding beacon was that failure was never an option; that I would prevail not only for myself but also for those behind, beside, and even in front of me, should they falter. It seemed I was destined to become "the exception," defying all the stereotypes associated with who I appeared to be to that club in which I would never really attain full membership. I endured lifelong pressure, especially when I sometimes was the first and often was the only one (Black and/or woman) in the room. I developed coping mechanisms early: mental, physical, and emotional, which worked well, until they didn't. Then, one day I finally broke through the tape at the finish line of what always felt to me like the hundred-yard dash—liberated and free for the first time to breathe and pursue my passions: to stop running that dash; instead, letting go and embracing the present—the period indicated by the line between the years of birth and death—fully living in my dash.

I have two younger brothers, Bruce Anthony Fitz born in 1959 and Neal David Fitz, born in 1967. Bruce and I shared many childhood experiences and memories, as I was not quite four years older than he. I was twelve when Neal was born, and I left for college when he was

Bruce, Neal, and Lauri, circa 1967

only five years old. When my brother Bruce was upset with me, he called me "Norma," a female version of our father Norman. Perhaps I had inherited this life rhythm from my father. Dad did, after all, attend Howard University on a track scholarship, and his race was the hundred-yard dash. He was a sprinter in every aspect of his life, constantly on the run, and not at home very often when we were growing up. He made time for his two passions—tennis and acting. He appeared happiest when he donned his tennis clothes and gathered his racket and balls, or when, throughout my preteen and teen years, he asked me to "cue his lines" as he prepared for a part in *Hamlet, Othello, Antigone, John Brown's Body,* or *Driving Miss Daisy.* For several years in the 1990's, he spent a lot of time in Baltimore acting in the television series *Homicide: Life on the Streets.*

Although Dad had been an athlete in high school and college, he didn't start playing tennis until college. Despite that late start, and just as he was determined to be a self-made man, he also developed a distinctive tennis game. He was fast and agile, physically and mentally. One

Dad in *Antigone*. *Ink drawing by Charles Mills, photographer Edward C. Jones*

of his longtime tennis friends described him as seeing what others couldn't—like Wayne Gretzky's famous saying, "skating to where the puck is going to be," Dad was a master at anticipating where the tennis ball would land.

He was a fierce competitor and when his energy waned, often won matches with mere grit and endurance, even against star athletes of the day like Boston Celtics basketball team great, Sam Jones. Jones took up tennis while still in Boston and had the bad luck of playing against my dad in an American Tennis Association tournament. He lost and their competition and friendship continued over many years. They discovered that Jones, from Wilmington, North Carolina, was married to a woman from Ahoskie, North Carolina, home of some of my father's relatives. Later in his life, when he became a member of the Edgemoor Club in Bethesda, Maryland, Dad met and played with other athletes, former players with the Washington Redskins, Sonny Jurgensen and Lonnie Sanders, who after leaving the football field, tried their hand at tennis. He was a formidable opponent for them all. Without the benefit of years of skills development and coaching, he still became a ranked amateur tennis player well into his '70s.

In the 1950s, tennis was not the sport of choice, nor was it accessible for a Black person. That was the era when Black tennis players created the American Tennis Association and when the US Tennis Association had a prohibition against Black players competing in their tournaments. Althea Gibson (who surprisingly played two sports, golf and tennis, although rarely were both mentioned in the same sentence when describing her) was among the first Black athletes to cross the international color line in tennis in 1956 when she won a Grand Slam at the French Championship, and in 1957, both Wimbledon and the US Nationals (now known as the US Open). These tennis players excelled half a century before the incredible sisters, Serena and Venus Williams, and a quarter of a century before the amazing Arthur Ashe, a friend of my dad's.

Tennis and acting required major time and practice and were my dad's passions; his day job clearly was not, although it was how he supported his family. Black men of that era often worked at jobs to support the family, despite the work being beneath their qualifications, rewarding or not, or "just a job." I was lucky enough to have parents with respected professions, who always worked, and who were exceptional contributors to our family's well-being.

My parents were first-generation college graduates who met at Howard University in 1951. Mom had no trouble passing the "brown bag" test, formally or informally applied as the color benchmark criterion for entry at several of the more desirable Black schools in Washington, DC. Dad, slightly darker skinned with grey eyes, had come from a small southern town where all shades of Black people were likely treated equally badly, given the infamous "one drop rule."*

---

*Any person with even one Black ancestor is considered Black.

Dad majored in zoology and was an actor in the renowned university theater group, The Howard Players, where one participant was the incomparable Toni Morrison. As much as he loved acting—unlike Sydney Poitier, James Earl Jones, Harry Belafonte, Ossie Davis, Ruby Dee and a couple of others of that era—very few aspiring Black actors could risk or afford to undertake the struggle to make it to the top. By the way, my father's low, deep, and melodious voice is in a dead heat with that of James Earl Jones.

While Dad was rarely at home, Mom was always there for us; she was our rock. Never a member of social clubs, she had only a few close girlfrie nds while we were growing up. She did not like being out in the heat, and, therefore, did not attend many of Dad's tennis tournaments. She was an avid reader, and any spare time was spent with family or with books.

At Howard University, my mother majored in Education and minored in Spanish. She became a devoted public-school English teacher. She loved the English language and foreign languages, international travel, and ballet. She also had dreams for her children, and especially for me, the only girl and the eldest of three. She instilled in me a passion for many of the things she loved but was unable to do during the times in which she grew up, or as a woman who became a wife and mother soon after graduating university. She encouraged me to read, to study, and to travel. I began studying Spanish at public school in third grade and developed an early interest in other cultures.

Dad pursued his passions and served as an example to help me follow my own; Mom exposed me to new ideas and experiences and facilitated and guided me on a journey to identify and pursue my own path. She encouraged me to see the world, to pursue a profession that would incorporate those things she exposed me to and that I embraced. For example, to feed my desire to see the world, she suggested I become a stewardess (one of a few professional options for women of color), and to remain focused on my ballet training while maintaining my grades in school, as my dad would not allow me to attend ballet class unless my grades were stellar. Even in those early years of my life a half-century ago, I knew this path was not the norm for a young colored girl. Maybe the novelty was not so evident given my father's atypical path—tennis and classical theatre.

In addition to ballet (as lily white as tennis), which played such a large role in my life, I was also exposed to theater and travel, alongside the struggles of integration in the North and the lessons of surviving in the segregated South. I had the unparalleled opportunity to experience foreign travel at a young impressionable age, which has helped me remain grounded in world affairs and always deeply aware of my privilege. I do appreciate that some among my Black female peers may have had some similar experiences, particularly if they were members of Jack and Jill, an elite social club for Black children where they learned social graces, participated in cotillions, and mingled with the "right" families. Many of those children formed lasting and beneficial friendships that were deepened with their later engagements in the Links or in Black sororities. I have many female and male friends who are part of the *divine nine* sororities and fraternities; I respect and appreciate the value of those networks. However, my parents were never joiners. Sure, Dad was a member of tennis organizations and the actor's union, but he and Mom believed that conformity was not the only road to success. They found ways to place us children strategically in schools, sports, and the arts, and hoped "the road less traveled" would distinguish us, make us more resilient, and ensure we became high achievers.

Mom and Dad, circa 2008

Over my more than half-century on this earth, I've had experiences that were fulfilling, enriching, transformational, and even harrowing, but each has been absolutely invaluable. What truly feeds my passion, though, is dance. What brings me peace, sustains me when little else can, and is a constant reminder of the symbiotic relationship between physical and mental agility, is dance.

Even recognizing the essential role it played for three decades of my life, my connection and involvement with dance ceased for a period of time when I was preoccupied with life's challenges and opportunities—marriage, raising the two children I gained when I married, and the daughter I gave birth to, a divorce . . . all while running those hundred-yard dashes. I rarely attended dance performances in those years; they were too difficult to watch. I had lost sight of this critical passion that had been the foundation of what made me successful, and that had taught me discipline, perseverance, musicality and strength. Dance had always fed my soul, but for a long moment its light had dimmed.

While my affinity for things international was integral to my professional life, as my journey continued, ballet returned as my anchor. With the consistency of practicing technique at the barre, followed by center floor adagio, allegro and pirouette combinations, and the understanding of the French terminology, I realized that I could take a ballet class anywhere in the world and feel challenged and fulfilled. I've learned, too, that physical and mental discipline accompanies muscle memory. So it is that for the last ten years, I have returned to adult classes several times a week in DC or wherever I travel.

I crave the rush of concluding a dance class feeling rejuvenated, having enjoyed the music and the rigor of always seeking precision and grace. I depart drenched in sweat and content that I still can find that special place, that escape from everything and everyone for 90 minutes. Reengaging with that lifelong comfort zone, that space of passion, allows me to emerge better able to handle all else that life has to offer.

Who knew that this place of peace would have started for me, at five years old in New York, when Mom enrolled me in Saturday ballet class just as I had started kindergarten in Mrs. Epstein's class at PS 140 in Jamaica, Queens. I wore a round green tag around my neck that signified my school bus stop, and I always tried to stand in line in front of or behind my friend, Michael Phipps, (his bus tag was red) as we marched into class and stood to say the pledge of allegiance to the flag.

Every time I hear "White Christmas," the song to which we danced in my first ballet recital in 1960, each movement, the lyrics, and music return to me as clear as "sleigh bells in the snow." It was a few years later, after we moved to DC in 1962, that I began serious ballet classes at the legendary Jones-Haywood Ballet School. Little did I know then that ballet would become so integral to my life.

In my experience, no species of performing artist is as self-critical as a dancer.

Part of being a dancer is this sometimes cruelly self-punishing objectivity about oneself, about one's shortcomings, as viewed from the perspective of an ideal observer, one more exacting than any real spectator could ever be . . .

—Susan Sontag, review of "Dancer and the Dance,"
by Lincoln Kirstein,

London Review of Books,
Vol. 9, No. 3, February 5, 1987

*****

Before the birth of the moon

We shed our social clothes.

Those false skins that we wear to reduce friction in a cruel and uncaring world.

Before the birth of the moon,

we were left struggling to stand in our beautiful and ugly truths

We stepped out of those heavy skins and revealed our nakedness, our unvarnished truths, our hopes, joys, our fears, our tribulations, our vulnerabilities, our guilts, our shames, our tangled and tattered histories

We stood in that tragic gap and went deep into painful places that rarely see the light of day.

So easy to surrender to the never-ending undercurrents carried in the wake of life. Victory is not getting clear of the turbulence, but finding the determination to go on swimming against the tide.

The journey is messy and so misunderstood by most. No matter, you are affirming the ancient wisdom that the unexamined life is not worth living.

—Robert L. Adams, Jr.

CHAPTER TWO

Agon

Every pew at the famous Riverside Church in New York City was full on that serene October evening in 2018 as we celebrated the life of Arthur Mitchell, famed New York City Ballet principal dancer and founder of the Dance Theatre of Harlem (DTH). Each speaker, dancer, and video clip weaved together awe-inspiring pieces of the history of his life and his contribution to the often unknown and deeply undervalued story of the legacy of Blacks in ballet in America. Among the pieces so stunningly performed in tribute to him was one from the ballet, *Agon*. I wondered how many of the hundreds gathered knew the story of that iconic pas de deux.

In 1957, at the City Center of Music and Drama, a groundbreaking ballet debuted for twelve dancers, with music by Igor Stravinsky and choreography by George Balanchine. The unprecedented part of *Agon* is the pas de deux, originally choreographed for Arthur Mitchell and Diana Adams, a Black man and a white woman. The audience was astounded. It is a beautiful and intimate piece, choreographed to contrast the stark difference of the complexions of the couple in its intricate movements.

Arthur Mitchell at The Washington Ballet School studio

The press coverage in the *New York Times* reflected the historic significance of the piece not only because of Balanchine's masterful choreography and Stravinsky's excellent score "but also because of its daring imagery." This was the first time in the United States that an American professional ballet company had featured a Black man and a white woman in a "breathtakingly intimate and masterfully sensual dance for two," as stated in a *New York Times* review.

I will always cherish the day in Washington, DC, in 2017, when I saw Arthur Mitchell for the last time. He walked assisted by a cane after a recent surgery and participated in an "in studio" master coaching session, organized by The Washington Ballet's Artistic Director, Septime Webre. Sitting in a chair, he commanded the room, as always, with his regal posture and ever-critical eye. He conducted an open master coaching session in which he critiqued two highly accomplished star Washington Ballet dancers, Brooklyn Mack and Maki Onuki, as if they were in a rehearsal to perform the famous *Agon* pas de deux. Its historic significance may have been lost or unknown to many in the audience, but not to me.

Arthur Mitchell had a paying audience seated in bleachers and chairs in the makeshift studio, so his customary acerbic tone was modulated as he delivered his oral "notes." Numerous times, he ordered the dancers to repeat the movements when not executed to his satisfaction. I marveled at his ability to direct the two dancers and ultimately to transform their technical execution into pure, divine art. The magic of Mitchell's instructive words and gestures took their performance to another level, capturing the musicality, emotion, and nuances of the movement far beyond their initial interpretation. It was awe inspiring to me and the others in attendance that day; we were grateful for the opportunity to witness so closely the significance of the history and artistry of that session.

A year later, during an unforgettable evening in Abu Dhabi, I was fascinated by the stories shared over cocktails by Tania León, a renowned Afro-Cuban American composer and conductor. She was a founding member and first musical director of the Dance Theatre of Harlem, sharing her tremendous musical gifts by composing the music for signature company works. Tania shared that Stravinsky drew much of his inspiration from Black jazz musicians that he listened to while frequenting a number of clubs in Harlem. Tania noted how influential jazz is in the music for *Agon*. It appears that *Agon* was even more daring and prescient than I had known. Balanchine, Stravinsky, Mitchell, and Adams artfully broke barriers, challenged stereotypes, and quietly revolutionized ballet long before more recent attempts at acceptance and inclusion of dancers of color.

Former Dance Theatre of Harlem principal dancer and DC native, Virginia Johnson, now expertly directs the DTH. When Virginia was studying at The Washington Ballet School, in the early stages of her performance

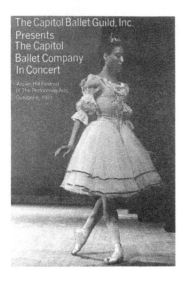

Sandra Fortune on the cover
of the Capitol Ballet program

experience, on occasion she danced with us at The Capitol
Ballet Company, the performing arm of the Jones-Haywood
Ballet School. The Company was a rigorous training ground
for many Jones-Haywood students, and primarily Black
dancers (there were a few white dancers in the school and
the dance company) around the country, preparing many
for professional ballet careers.

Those of us who studied at Jones-Haywood couldn't
have imagined at that point that we would one day take
current students at the school to New York to see DTH
perform or see a few of them selected to train at DTH's
summer intensive dance program. We, who were around
to appreciate the significance of DTH's birth, first in a
space at a church, and later in a garage at 466 West 152nd
Street, were fearful when, for lack of funding, the company was forced into an eight-year hiatus. Ballet schools
and companies are often challenged by securing sufficient funding and by efficient operations management,
both of which are essential for survival of dance schools
and companies.

Claire Haywood, *left,* and
Doris Jones

After we moved to Washington, DC, my mother found
me a new ballet home at Jones-Haywood School of Ballet.
The school was founded by two African American wom-
en, Doris Jones and Claire Haywood, who were committed
to providing dance training, order, standards, and discipline to Black children. Doris Jones, who was from Boston
and maintained that distinctive accent until her death,
aspired to be a ballet dancer when there was little opportunity for a child of color to study ballet in this country.
The story we heard from Miss Jones was that as a child
she couldn't attend segregated dance classes, so she was
taught by a rare white teacher who gave her private instruction after her white students had left for the day. An
accomplished tap dancer, she taught tap classes on occasion in exchange for ballet lessons. Claire Haywood was
born in Atlanta, Georgia, and, at one time, had been a student of Miss Jones. We knew little else about her although
we saw some of her impressive paintings in their home.

We ballet classmates have stories of our many experiences at Jones-Haywood that we have preserved as lore for

generations to come. We share tears of laughter and some pain as we recall the "old school" strict training and "the rod," or more accurately the cane, of one of our teachers. It was tough love often accompanied by harsh criticism, which made most of us stronger and more determined to persevere and succeed in the dance studio and in life. Claire Haywood and Doris Jones were best described in a 1974 Capitol Ballet program, "They believed the rigorous dance training and techniques are strongly complemented by intellectual as well as aesthetic development and growth, character building, the constant quest for proficiency leadership ability, faith, dedication to hard work, and discipline 'the steel holding the bridge together."

We alumni of Jones-Haywood from that era are so proud of our contemporaries and former classmates who have been able to carve out successful professional careers on stage and off. Hinton Battle, who studied with us as a young boy, received the same Ford Foundation scholarship several of us did, and was able later to move to New York to attend the intense program at the School of American Ballet. Hinton performed in award-winning Broadway shows, became a director and choreographer, and now has opened dance schools in Japan. The students clamor to learn from him and his instructors, fascinated with the training in traditional as well as the ever-evolving newer genres that they offer. In fact, many African American-created or -influenced styles of dance have been emulated, adopted, and popularized, both domestically and globally.

Arthur Mitchell made several unexpected appearances in my life that have deeply impacted me. While that day in Washington, DC, in 2017 was the last, the first was when I was a young ballet student at that groundbreaking dance school for Black children.

I have never heard the full story but know that George Balanchine, the Russian who transformed ballet in Amer-

From left: Lauri, Joyce Mosso Stokes, Hinton Battle and Lynne Breece

ica, took an interest in Doris Jones and Claire Haywood. He not only mentored them but also provided the opportunity for several of us to receive scholarships from the Ford Foundation to pay for our training at Jones-Haywood. Even though some foundation funding was linked to ensuring diverse participation, many of his actions truly went beyond what was required or assumed. I remain curious about reconciling what was widely coined the "Balanchine Ballerina": thin and uniform, with his actions in support of Black dancers. Perhaps Daniel Duell, City Ballet principal and husband of famed City Ballet favorite Kyra Nichols, explained it best in the *New York Times* article, "The Creation of a Balanchine Ballerina":

> ... the *"Balanchine dancer"* is a state of mind. "A lot of dancers who do not fit the image have gone a long way in the company," he says. "I think Balanchine admires people who do not lead safe lives, who don't take refuge

in diligence or technique for its own sake. A whole
realm of people who have something special."

—*New York Times*, February 8,
1981, Section 2, page 1

Visiting our school several times, and after selecting the group of us who received the School of American Ballet scholarships, Balanchine dispatched the second Black male dancer at New York City Ballet to check on our progress and to teach us on occasion—the inimitable Arthur Mitchell, who, after the assassination of Martin Luther King, Jr., felt an urgency to create the Dance Theatre of Harlem. He knew it was time to advance the groundbreaking opportunity Balanchine had given him, and launched DTH with Balanchine's endorsement and support.

"In 1933, the dancer Lincoln Kirstein wrote a letter to
a director in Hartford, Connecticut introducing his new
friend, Balanchine, and their joint aspirations to start
a ballet. [Sic] Kirstein called for a core of "16 dancers,
half women, half men, half white and half negro." What
resulted was the creation of the School of American
Ballet and New York City Ballet, founded by Kirstein
and Balanchine. However, their joint plan for student
diversity was never realized: Administrative forces
that opposed the idea of an integrated ballet company
consistently blocked them."

—"In Ballet, Blacks Are Still Chasing a Dream of
Diversity," *New York Times*, May 7, 2007

That Mr. B (as he was respectfully called by many) supported people of color is a little acknowledged subject. Few today remember that Mr. B was once married to the beautiful Native American prima ballerina, Maria Tallchief.

One unforgettable story Mr. Mitchell recounted at that same *Agon* master coaching session at The Washington

Ballet was about his time on tour with City Ballet. Mitchell said Balanchine would not allow company members to stay at facilities that shunned him whenever there was alternative lodging available. Indeed, Balanchine and City Ballet blazed a trail for Black ballet dancers in America when support for Black performers was not commonplace.

> *Dance demands a degree of service greater than in any other performing art, or sport. While the daily life of every dancer is a full-time struggle against fatigue, strain, natural physical limitations and those due to injuries (which are inevitable), dance itself is the enactment of an energy, which must seem, in all respects, untrammeled, effortless, masterful and at every moment fully mastered. The dancer's performance smile is not so much a smile as simply a categorical denial of what he or she is actually experiencing – for there is some discomfort, and often pain, in every major stint of performing. This is an important difference between the dancer and the athlete, who have much in common (ordeal, contest, brevity of career). In sport, the signs of effort are not concealed: on the contrary, making effort visible is part of the display. The public expects to see, and is moved by, the spectacle of the athlete visibly pushing himself or herself beyond the limits of endurance.*
>
> —Susan Sontag, "Dancers and the Dance,"
> *London Review of Books*, Vol. 9, No.3, February 5, 1987

We were driven so hard at ballet school that we dance students found refuge among ourselves and formed a protective family unit. I learned along the way that often Jones-Haywood was an escape from dysfunction in our own homes. As young as we were, some students were suffering the repercussions of domestic violence, drugs and alcohol, physical and emotional abuse, and neglect.

In fact, a few of us, generally some of the boys who were struggling from a lack of nutrition, found that it was at the school that they were sure to enjoy a decent meal. Jones-Haywood became more of a home to many of the students than their own. Maybe this sense of refuge is why the late evening classes, all-day Saturday schedules for the younger students, rehearsals late into the evenings, or even Sunday sessions preparing for a performance, were not viewed as excessive by the students, then or now.

Our lives revolved around that white building attached to the two-story house with the large living room and office on the first floor and the living quarters upstairs. We rarely saw the living quarters unless we were summoned upstairs for a talk. That usually meant bad news, and always involved a conversation with Miss Haywood or Miss Jones about poor performance in class or something else that concerned them. We much preferred entering the side entrance and descending the few steps to our metal lockers in the girls' locker room where we placed our schoolbooks and school clothes.

As we changed into our dance leotards and tights, making sure our hair was properly combed and brushed off our face into a neat bun, we chatted about our day at school, a new boyfriend, the boys in the dressing room next door, or simply laughed with each other about the sweet torture to come. We protected each other from the prospect of not living up to the expectations of our teachers. We worked especially hard not to reveal any activities that were contrary to the rules they had put in place. We knew we were not to play any sports because they developed the wrong muscles or could result in injuries; we could not become cheerleaders at school nor have a boyfriend without our teachers deriding us about it in class.

We remained each other's accomplices, the holders of secrets, and did all we could to ensure none of our transgressions would escape our lips. In fact, two of our group had indeed become cheerleaders, and we made sure that our teachers never saw them enter the building in their uniforms, and we often helped hide their pom-poms in our lockers. We even tried to keep from our teachers the fact that several of us had serious boyfriends who waited for us to finally emerge from the building, always later than everyone else, so our teachers would be none the wiser. We learned to read Miss Haywood's mood from the color of the pantsuit she wore to class (I never saw her in a dress). Our teachers were demanding, discerning, had expensive tastes, and didn't hesitate to express their preferences. Claire Haywood told us at holiday time that if we were giving them anything, the only fragrance they would wear was Estee Lauder. Even today, we use some of the nicknames they gave us and that we gave each other: Pun'kin, NewbyAnne, Lynnie, Fitzie, Joycie, and Hinty.

As I was the youngest among the group of more senior dancers, I learned a lot from them about the facts of life. They were the older sisters I never had at a time when a two- or three-year age difference was meaningful. The dancers at Jones-Haywood were my dearest friends, providing me with the kind of intimate relationship that I could not have with my white girlfriends at school. From the girls at ballet school, I learned early the necessity of mutual trust, the importance of keeping secrets, and how to be selective about revealing information that might come back to haunt me.

Doris Jones and Claire Haywood exposed us to the world of incredible and internationally renowned choreographers. When famous guest choreographers like Louis Johnson, George Faison, or Billy Wilson, all with Jones-Haywood training themselves, came back to "set" a dance piece for the Capitol Ballet Company to perform, we were all nervous and excited. We also knew that we

Lauri performing with Capitol Ballet, circa 1972

had better not make mistakes that reflected badly on our teachers. When they descended those wooden steps or sat observing from a seat on the steps, like Miss Jones often did when we were learning the choreography, we worked even harder to capture every step, arm movement, and angle of the head.

It was so important to us that we not disappoint our teachers. When it was time to be fitted for our costumes, we ate less that day to ensure that we had a "skinny day." As conscious as we are now in the age of body positivity, as girls in ballet school, we often looked at ourselves in the small mirror over the sink in the dressing room before scurrying into class, and remarked to each other, "Uh oh, this is a fat day." We hoped that on our "fat days," we wouldn't be called over to Miss Haywood's stool near the piano where we were told to step on the scale. As we grew and our bodies changed, some of us became aware that we had expanded in all the wrong places. Unlike today, when people have finally stopped insisting on traditional, classic, thin, Balanchine bodies for ballet dancers, we were held to the traditional standards and expectations without the benefits of such things as Pilates reformers, weight training, stretching classes, and physical therapy. We also were expected to work through the pain of bleeding toes, cracked soles, and aching muscles. And yet, we did not suffer from bulimia, anorexia, or other unfortunate diseases that many dancers struggle to overcome; our close bonds, support systems, and sheer laughter kept us healthy and somewhat sane.

The bonds we developed at dance school were so tight that it was my dance partner, Leroy Cowan, who took me to my high school prom when my boyfriend, Ailue Gunter, who had previously graduated from B-CC High School and was then a Morehouse man wouldn't. Another dancer, Rodney Green, dressed Leroy for the evening (a bit creatively when you consider that the event was held at a stodgy country club). I never discovered whose car he was driving when he picked me up, and it was even more of a miracle that he got me safely to the club and then back home again given his limited driving skills!

Leroy Cowan was not only there in ballet class to lift me, catch me, and steady me when I balanced on one foot during multiple partnered turns and pirouettes, but in addition to taking me to the prom, he also walked me to the bus stop a block down and across the street from our ballet school on dark nights to take the bus for my hour-long bus ride home. Soon after we moved to Silver Spring, I had begun going to ballet class alone by public bus several days a week and on Saturdays. My routine began in the afternoons after Mom returned home from the school where she taught and I arrived home from my school, and we would sit to watch one of her daily soap operas, either her recorded *As the World Turns*, which aired during her school day, or *The Edge of Night*.

I would then walk the two blocks, the second of which was a steep hill that became a special challenge in rain or snow, to the bus stop on Georgia Avenue. I had to transfer to another bus at the downtown Silver Spring bus station. The entire one-way trip to Jones-Haywood took more than an hour, and that was only if there weren't bus delays. Some winter evenings, when the darkness came early or it was very cold, I really would have loved to stay at home in my room, curled up in bed, doing my homework, taking a nap, or reading a book, all while listening to The Delfonics on my record player. Despite these moments of weakness, I rarely missed a class. I knew my teachers and friends at dance school expected that I would be there; I also had strong expectations for myself that I would be disciplined, focused, and a high achiever in every aspect of my life. Besides, we were all in this together, my ballet friends and me. We worked hard, loved our craft, and were good at it. We lifted each other up.

Those with a license and access to a car often drove miles out of their way after late rehearsals to take me to my home, which may have been among the furthest from the studio. We still laugh about the night the girls drove me home after a particularly late rehearsal then decided it was best to go into the house with me, anticipating that I would be in trouble with my very strict father because I'd returned home so late on a school night. They explained that I was late because of a guest choreographer teaching us a new piece. His response, in his booming bass voice was, "I don't care if Sydney Poitier was there. Lauri knows what time she is supposed to be in this house." Sandra Fortune-Green still loves to tell that story, although she's barely able to get the words out between peals of laughter.

Dad also never hesitated to speak his mind to my dance teachers, sometimes to my great dismay as I feared the collateral damage to me. One particular incident still stands out for me. After I graduated from high school and went to Vassar College in Poughkeepsie, New York, I had returned on occasion to perform with Jones-Haywood's performing company. While I was in Spain for my college junior year abroad, I found out much to my chagrin that Dad had confronted Miss Haywood about compensation for a movie in which several of us Capitol Ballet dancers had appeared, *Sincerely the Blues*, produced by Baker Morton, which aired at a theater in DC while I was in Madrid. The movie told the story of the birth and development of the blues. We danced in four pieces choreographed by Doris Jones. Dad saw the movie and believed that we dancers should have been compensated for our work. He had a lawyer write an aggressively worded and somewhat threatening letter demanding compensation for me and the other dancers, confident that Jones-Haywood had received some remuneration for having its students appear in the movie.

It didn't go so well for Dad, who met his match in Miss Haywood. It was apparent she was "time enough for him" from her well-developed response to the letter. I didn't learn about this controversy until my return home from Madrid. In fact, I recently found the letters the two of them exchanged, and I chuckled at the feistiness on both sides. Miss Haywood died in 1978, two years after that exchange, and a year after I graduated from college. I can still hear her voice during rehearsals of *Rhapsody in Blue*, the last piece I performed with the company. "You must be learning something at that college." I can still hear her voice as she commented in an audible whisper to Jonesie, as she called Miss Jones, "Look at that new sass in her movements, Jonesie," then turned to me and said, "Aw, sell it, girl."

When we reached that serious stage of our dance training around the age of twelve or thirteen, we spent every evening and most of Saturday at "the studio" or, as one student's boyfriend called it, the "spin house." Every former student of the school that I have ever met, no matter their profession, gives major credit for who they are today to that school—first, to Miss Jones and Miss Haywood, if they are old enough to have been guided by both, or after Miss Haywood passed, by only Miss Jones who continued to run the school until she died in 2006, and later to the guardians of the legacy who succeeded our founders. Jones-Haywood's alumni, no matter their generation, are grateful for not only the quality dance training we received but also the lasting friendships we developed, and finally, for the deep and abiding life skills and lessons learned.

The school celebrated its 80th year in 2021. The current artistic director, installed in 2007, is Sandra Fortune-Green, Jones-Haywood's own prima ballerina, who worked harder than anyone else in our group to be her best, and whose mastery of technique and unrelenting determination took her to international competitions in Moscow and twice in Varna, Bulgaria. Sandra is among the elite corps of Black ballerinas to have competed and placed in an international ballet competition in her time. She was the first African American ballerina to compete in Moscow. At home in Washington, DC, Mary Day, the director of the city's National Ballet professional dance company, later renamed The Washington Ballet, appeared on (as my mother liked to say) "national color TV" and said Black bodies are not suited to ballet. The world of dance may still have a long way to go in crafting its narrative around Black agency in classical ballet, but clearly, Sandra had already debunked that myth overseas at international competitions and then in Washington when she joined The Washington Ballet briefly in the late 1970s.

In the early years of her career, Sandra was partnered with and coached by the handsome and highly accomplished Sylvester Campbell, then with the Royal Netherlands Ballet, for competition at the seventh Varna, Bulgaria, International Ballet Competition. The Capitol Ballet Guild, the managing body of the Capitol Ballet

Company was conceived in 1957 by the parents of students at Jones-Haywood. With the performing arm of the school finally established in 1962, First Lady Jacqueline Kennedy contributed a small etching to sell at its first fund-raising event.

In a press release upon the return of Sandra and Sylvester from the Varna competition, the Guild stated:

> *"Sandra Fortune and Sylvester Campbell are local talents. It marks an historic event that Sandra is the first black girl to pass the third round and win any type of award in the history of World Ballet Competition.*
>
> *The Capitol Ballet is proud that Sandra has broken the barriers of a white-dominated art and has become the first black ballerina of this country, and thus has opened the doors to black children over the nation."*

While calling her the "first black ballerina of this country" was a bit of hyperbole, Jones-Haywood continues to be respected as the birthplace of many firsts and has earned a highly respected place in the world of dance.

Sandra and Sylvester's performance of the beautiful and haunting Le Corsaire pas de deux is my favorite. Loosely based on Lord Byron's epic poem, "The Corsaire," it is a romantic tale of pirates, slaves, and intrigue. The most celebrated part of the ballet is the Le Corsaire pas de deux, also among classical ballet's most performed excerpts. It has been described as containing "logic-defying leaps and stunning endless turns of dancers who've trained their bodies into peak physical condition." Her classmates and friends at Jones-Haywood watched in awe as Sandra trained and rehearsed endlessly with the cajoling and taunting of Miss Jones and Miss Haywood. During those long days and nights, as many of us held our collective breath for Sandra as she stretched, jumped, and practiced her thirty-two fouetté turns, day after day, we also recall the sound of the cane as it beat out the rhythm, or demanded endless repetition of a step, a position, a pirouette, and the steady rise and fall of the voices of our directors, and then, only once or twice, one or the other might call her by her nickname "Pun'kin" and give the occasional compliment. Our little group just looked on and swooned; for most of us, Sylvester may have been among the first Black professional ballet dancers we had seen in the flesh, and we, Sandra's cheering squad, knew we were privileged to watch them rehearse and perform. Miss Haywood often told us when she was dissatisfied with a rehearsal, or simply wanted to browbeat us into pushing ourselves harder, "The only people who are going to applaud that mess, are your five friends in the audience." We still laugh and refer to our tight knit group as "the five friends."

Sandra and a group of us grew up in a cigarette smoke-filled studio as both of our instructors were heavy smokers. It was common to see Miss Haywood holding a cigarette between her lips as she adjusted our bodies. We knew nothing about the dangers of secondhand smoke then, and this was likely instrumental in my extreme sensitivity to cigarette smoke now.

We performed at Lisner Auditorium on George Washington University's campus, at Howard University's Cramton Auditorium, traveled on occasion to other Historically Black Colleges and Universities, and even performed at one of President Nixon's Inaugural parties—what formative and incredible experiences for our group of innocents. Mrs. Nixon even honored Sandra, presenting her with a bouquet of red roses after a performance at the Smithsonian's Museum of Natural History upon her return from Moscow with her partner Clover Mathis (an Alvin Ailey dancer), her first international competition.

When the magnificent John F. Kennedy Center for the Performing Arts opened in Washington, DC, in 1971, Leonard Bernstein's *Mass* christened the opera house

From left: Kennedy Center official, First Lady Patricia Nixon, Claire Haywood, Doris Jones, and Sandra Fortune, *Capitol Ballet newsletter*

with its musical theatre extravaganza. I was sixteen when I auditioned and was selected to dance in *Beatrix Cenci*, an opera in two acts by Alberto Ginastra, which also debuted as part of the Kennedy Center opening on September 10, 1971. What an exciting opportunity it was to perform in elaborate, gorgeous but heavy period dresses, with corset-like bodices and full long billowing skirts lined with endless yards of itchy material. We performed elegant "court dancing" in heels on a raked stage (a stage that slopes upward) choreographed by Joyce Trisler. I loved the new experience and with Sandra Fortune (also selected from Jones-Haywood) explored the areas backstage, and every entrance and exit of the majestic new building. During our breaks, we watched rehearsals of the *Mass* and checked on my brother Bruce and Miss Jones' nephew who were cast as young extras.

The school continues in full operation as it approaches its 80th anniversary. The house the school occupies stands well worn and proudly on Delafield Place with the same single studio attached, and with a full complement of children enrolled. In fact, among the students today are grandchildren of the girls I met in class many years ago. If Miss Jones and Miss Haywood were still with us, they could boast that three generations of children have passed through those doors.

As I look back on that time, I realize how fortunate I am that my mother found Jones-Haywood. As the years went by, the students there became the recipients of so many unprecedented opportunities. One such student was Chita Rivera, who Miss Jones took by train to New York for an audition that Mr. B attended at the School of American Ballet. Not only did she do well in that audition but is now in her 80s and still performing in a one woman show in New York. While she has many Broadway credits, I think of her "killing it" playing the role of "Anita" in the Jerome Robbins-choreographed, groundbreaking original *West Side Story* on Broadway. I look forward to seeing the newly released modern version of *West Side Story*, on Broadway after the COVID-19 shut down, but doubt its impact could be the same as that of the original. A few years ago, our Jones-Haywood alumni committee invited Chita Rivera to a fund-raiser we organized for the school where Hinton Battle choreographed the students in a tribute to her to the music "Big Spender." She was so gracious and encouraging, even giving the girls a standing ovation.

Many other Jones-Haywood students have gone on to illustrious careers in the field of dance and theater over many generations: Lewis Johnson, Hope Clarke, George Faison, Charles Augins, Renee Robinson, and Dionne Figgins, to name a few. Their stellar training was always the reason they found success in New York, in shows on tour, and abroad, with many like Chita Rivera achieving long-lasting success. Ironically, as a child, my mother often visited her twin cousins who grew up in the same neighborhood with the young Chita, when she was known as Delores Figaro.

Misty Copeland, perhaps the best-known Black principal ballerina of our time, stands on the shoulders of scores of famous and little-known Black ballerinas. Some fled to Europe for performance opportunities, and, if fair skinned enough, they even "passed" for white to gain ac-

Misty Copeland and Lauri

ceptance into elite ballet companies. Of course, far too many also gave up classical ballet to pursue careers in other more "acceptable" dance genres or related fields. Luckily for us, Misty arrived on the scene at just the right moment in time. She is beauty and grace, sweetness and strength, and she has achieved unprecedented heights with endorsement contracts and opportunities to represent companies from Coach to Under Armour. Not only have these corporate sponsors recognized the required athleticism of the toned professional dancer's body, but they have also acknowledged the fluidity and strength of a tiny 5'3" brown body to broadcast their products to the masses. Misty has become famous, with the expert advice of her superb manager, Gilda Squire, in an era of increased opportunity and access for people of color across the spectrum of business and culture.

Misty Copeland graced the halls of Jones-Haywood on a snowy January evening several years ago. She took time out of a hectic schedule while in Washington for performances with American Ballet Theatre at the Kennedy Center. A group of Jones-Haywood alumni sat for a chat with her before accompanying her to the studio where a few of our highly rehearsed students anxiously waited to perform. As she listened attentively to our stories about the school's founders, the barriers and the lack of opportunity, and the many obstacles placed along our paths to sustainable professional careers, in and outside of the field of dance, tears ran down her cheeks. Many of the young ballerinas there that night, and who today face few of the difficulties we faced in years gone by, will speak of Misty in hushed tones, as I still do when I speak of Arthur Mitchell. He is the icon of my youth; Misty is the icon of today.

In addition to the much-needed evolution of thought about inclusion of talented and deserving dancers of diverse backgrounds, the recent changes in the world of ballet are attributable to more equitable and holistic training, advanced physical therapy, cross training, and knowledge about nutrition. Further, the evolution of the traditional dance genre of ballet has brought recognition that Brown ballerinas work equally as hard to perfect the correct and aesthetically pleasing bodylines that are true to the rigorous ballet technique. In addition, brown skin-toned tights and pointe shoes provide a somewhat more level playing field for achieving the expected uninterrupted extension of the leg to the tip of the toe. Imagine the Black ballerinas who back in the day could only wear the available pink tights and footwear more appropriate to their white counterparts, or who more recently may have spent countless hours dabbing brown makeup on their pink pointe shoes to match the now available flesh tone tights. Today, we marvel at the young dancers who think nothing of searching an online catalog to select tights with footwear that match their skin tone.

One of these days, I'm going to buy a pair of those beautiful satin pointe shoes, in a hue to match my brown skin, and hang them on my wall to admire and to be reminded of how far classical ballet has come in this country—and how far it still has to go.

CHAPTER THREE

Grand Jeté

In our all-white neighborhood in Silver Spring, Maryland, where we moved when I was eleven years old and entered Montgomery Hills Junior High School, my middle brother Bruce attended Woodlyn Elementary School, and Neal was born at the end of the first year of our move. I used to babysit for the two Hannah boys, Matt and Jay (JB), who lived across the street. Their house was next door to another white family whose children peeped at my family from behind the trees in their yard, diagonally across the street from ours. They were convinced, said Lisa Green my next-door neighbor and schoolmate, that we might turn them into witches upon eye contact. Claudia Hannah, the boys' mother, was a Vassar graduate whose father had taught at the college for many years. She was the first to plant the seed about my attending college at Vassar in Poughkeepsie, New York. On many occasions when I came to babysit her sons, Matt and JB, the conversation included her recollections about her college experience and ended with her encouraging me to apply to her alma mater.

Claudia and my mother became close friends. Our

neighbor exuded an ever-present expression of awe, delight, and joy in every conversation with my family members. I never knew if she expressed herself the same way with everyone, or just with us. She was constantly amazed at our activities, travels, plans, and accomplishments. Appearing to take vicarious pleasure in our every move, she would hear about a development in my life and if I was at home when she stopped by, would pepper me with questions while towering all of her six feet over me in glorious joyfulness, like an awestruck child. After she and her husband divorced, she was the first person I knew to engage in the new dating service technology. I never found out which one she used, although I did learn that people were matched through videos. My mother kept me informed and was surprised at how successful Claudia was with the service, when after each usually long and gratifying relationship, she found a new mate. When Claudia died, her son Matt presided over the gathering of friends and family, and I learned about her life of service to community and progressive causes, academic achievements, and about her generosity of spirit; none of which was surprising for this avant-garde, Vassar-educated woman.

It gives me joy to observe the lasting friendship that developed between Matt and my brother Neal. Jay, Matt, and Neal grew up together. He became a quite accomplished drummer as a teenager and often jammed with the boys at the Hannah home. JB remained in the area and unfortunately died several years ago. Matt has been a professor in Germany for many years but returned to visit his Mom regularly until her death and continues to come back to town for annual visits. He, my brother, and a group of old neighborhood friends make a weekend trip to Ocean City every year. My father and I were equally surprised when we learned from the assembled posse of Neal's friends at the celebration of Claudia's life that Neal was considered the life of the party, the guy with the jokes that made everyone laugh until they cried. The only indication I have of his entertaining chops are memories of him as a tiny boy, pretending to hold a mic, and perfectly imitating the then popular singer from Wales who had a weekly television show with the words, *This Is Tom Jones*.

Neal has taught special needs students for over twenty years, primarily in Prince George's County, Maryland, schools. Neither of my brothers has married and Neal says if he ever does, he wants no children. It may be that his teaching experience has influenced this decision. I admire him deeply and am so grateful for the closer relationship we have developed in recent years as time and family crises gradually have closed our twelve-year age gap.

Bruce and I, with three and a half years between us, were very close in our teen years, and after a long hiatus, when I was married and he was experiencing his own challenges, we have recaptured the bond of our youth. He often accused me of escaping much of our father's tough and often emotionally paralyzing discipline and criticism, as well as household and yard chores, because I was rarely at home when we were growing up due to my ballet classes, rehearsals, and performances. I continuously assure him that, as the eldest, I received my share of opprobrium. Thankfully, our younger brother, Neal, experienced a relatively more mature and mellow father.

I paid for the privilege of attending ballet classes at Jones-Haywood by having to maintain excellent grades. I attended a middle school, Montgomery Hills Junior High, and one of the highest-ranked high schools in the country at the time, Bethesda-Chevy Chase High School (B-CC), through my father's creative thinking and connections. In those days, to transfer to an "out of district" school, special circumstances would have to be demonstrated. I don't know how he came up with it, but my father officially requested that I attend B-CC because I was a ballet dancer and needed to learn Russian. Did he think I was Bolshoi material? While Russian dancers are famous for their expertise, it would have taken only a small amount of research to discover that learning the Russian language would have done me no good at all, given that ballet terminology is in French, not Russian. Although this was the appeal my father submitted for my successful transfer to B-CC, I was spared from studying Russian because that year the class was discontinued. I took German in its place and studied both it and Spanish throughout high school. In fact, my two favorite teachers of all time were my Spanish teacher, Consuelo Eddy, and my German teacher, Barbara English.

My blond-haired blue-eyed best friend since seventh grade, Bob Kroll, a star basketball player, whose family gratefully emulated my father's formula to gain a transfer from Montgomery Blair High School to B-CC, also studied both languages. He never was great at either; we had already agreed that he was the math guy, and I was the English and foreign language girl. Together we made a killer academic pair, and we loved the perplexed reaction of our teachers, as we introduced ourselves as siblings, and alternated pointing out which one of us was adopted.

During that same period, upon the direction of my father, who early in my teens wanted me to diversify my exposure to the arts, I auditioned for the theater program at the George Washington University Workshop for Careers in the Arts. This was not the dance program, which might have been quite exciting that year, as Debbie Allen directed it. I will always remember Debbie Allen as the young dance instructor at the GW Workshop. She is the now-famous dance school owner, choreographer, producer, and actor in film and television (*Grey's Anatomy*) who played the dance teacher Lydia Grant in the iconic movie and television musical drama *Fame*. Despite all of that, when I think of Debbie Allen, my thoughts always go back to the George Washington Workshop.

Dad wanted me to study theater that summer, so I auditioned and was accepted into the drama program that was directed by the legendary Harry Poe. In his *Washington Post* obituary, it was said of Poe:

After years of directing, producing, acting and teaching theater in Washington, Poe had sent scores of students into show business . . . Poe started a theater and visual arts complex on Georgia Avenue NW called Gallery One and founded a black American film festival at the American Film Institute. He also worked with owners of the New Theatre of Washington, an upstart black company that merged with the half-century-old Washington Theatre Club, the first time in Washington history that black and white theaters were united.

I was surrounded and swallowed up by a tsunami of young Black talent, and that, along with my raging hormones, brought my most primal emotions to the surface. What a summer that was. Mike Malone ran the auditions for the street theater production *Everyman*, in which I landed the dance role of the "good Joan" and for which my Jones-Haywood classmate, Lyndell Walker, was selected as the "bad Joan." We performed the musical on street corners in Washington, DC, and on the grounds of New York City's Rockefeller Center. In countless ways, my experience in the GW program the summer before I entered high school was a precursor to Vassar and a coming-of-age. Back at Jones-Haywood, our ballet teachers, Claire Haywood and Doris Jones, were livid that three of us, Joyce Mattison, Lyndell Walker and I, had decided to spend the summer performing in a musical instead of continuing our ballet training with them. Despite that, the life lessons I gained—the opportunity to revisit DC neighborhoods in southeast DC, where I had lived as a child, and being in a comfortable sea of multitalented Black youth, would influence my confidence, development, education, and perceptions in indescribable ways. The depth of the weekly crushes, the drama, the incipient sexual feelings, and the genuine and mature love relationships, breakups, and makeups, all set against a backdrop of music, dance, and dialogue, blended seamlessly into the production's dramatic crying scenes in the rain.

That summer, many stars were born, lifelong relationships were formed, and dreams took flight. Regardless of the future path each one of us chose, that summer marked the formation of the impermeable core of the people we all would eventually become.

The GW Workshop was the forerunner to Washington DC's Duke Ellington School of the Arts, a public high school for talented and creative local students. When I entered the beautifully renovated school to teach ballet at the summer dance program in the summer of 2019, I saw the portraits of Peggy Cooper Cafritz and Mike Malone gracing the lobby and remembered that long ago summer at GW when they directed that groundbreaking program.

Peggy Cooper Cafritz was an arts and social change advocate whose work benefited so many and who is cherished throughout the city. She touched the lives of so many young people, particularly those of color in DC, through her commitment to the arts and education, and through her philanthropy. Raised in a well-to-do Black family in Mobile, Alabama, Peggy began college at George Washington University in 1964 where she organized a Black student union during a memorable period of civil rights history. She was an activist on campus and throughout her life, serving six controversial years on the DC school board. Always speaking her mind, her directness could take one by surprise, but her dedication and determination could never be questioned. Peggy lobbied vociferously to fund the renovation of the Duke

Ellington School of the Arts and was able to see her work realized before she died at age 70 in 2018. Fortunately, Peggy lived long enough to see the fruits of her labor to renovate and expand her beloved school. The magnificent Mike Malone, a director, teacher, and choreographer, and Duke Ellington's first artistic director, died in 2006, and, unfortunately, did not live to see the school fully come into its own. Peggy and Mike both opened unprecedented doors in Washington, DC, and nationally, leaving a legacy of valued achievements that will benefit future generations.

Today, I feel privileged to be part of that legacy, to have come full circle and to give back to the institution they created. The Duke Ellington School's Charles Augins, Dance Director, also a Jones-Haywood alum, has a history that few can rival as a dancer who conquered untouched territory with many white marquee stars of his times. He was among the talented young Black men, who, along with a few young Black women, reached heights perhaps unheralded, but nevertheless unheard of in their times, or in any time. On the talented and committed dance staff at Duke Ellington are two other Jones-Haywood alums, fellow Capitol Ballet members and longtime friends, and current artistic director at Jones-Haywood, Sandra Fortune-Green, and Adrian Vincent James.

Imagine the exhilaration and excitement I feel about those poignant memories from that summer almost fifty years ago. I feel such pride each time I enter the magnificent and beautifully renovated Duke Ellington School of the Arts. I hope the students today will learn about and appreciate the rich history coursing within the walls of their school. As I walk the halls, my mind and muscle memory create the image of a "grand jeté"—a big leap where the legs separate into a front split in the air, suspended in flight for a few seconds, before the dancer lands on one foot with the other leg trailing in the air behind.

I hit "fast forward" in my mind and reflect on the trajectory my life has taken with dance all these many years. I've always had a strong work ethic and have appreciated the balance necessary to enjoy the good things life has to offer, while ensuring that I have the means to take care of myself and to support my family. I've also worked from a young age—my first job at about fifteen years old was teaching ballet to the "little buddies," the four- and five-years-olds at Jones-Haywood, on Saturdays. That, and babysitting, were the ways I earned money while I was in high school. At Vassar, in addition to my parents' contribution, I received limited financial aid, always had a campus job, and paid back college loans well into my thirties.

Getting into Vassar College was magical, and not just because the inimitable Claudia Hannah conjured me there. I certainly felt the stars must have aligned with Claudia's wishes because a wonderful African American man from Vassar's admissions office, George Crowell (the only man of color working in that office at the time, as I understand it), came to recruit at my high school and continued my neighbor's hard sell. With an excellent academic record, I was accepted at several stellar east coast schools. In the era before parents began chauffeuring their children to visit numerous prospective schools, my parents and brothers delivered me to Vassar College sight unseen, and got me settled in my triple occupancy dorm room with Fran Pagano and Cindy Ornstein. Fran had the middle room, larger but with no privacy, because Cindy and I had to enter and exit through the one door in her room to reach our tiny rooms on either side of hers. Frannie and I developed a great relationship, and I was sorry to see her transfer to a school closer to her home after our freshman year.

Before exiting past the "white angel," the woman sit-

Joyce Mayes, graduation
from Howard University

ting at the dorm's front desk to monitor those coming
and going, Mom's last act, in my tiny sparse room, was
to make up my narrow bed with the new sheets and
bedspread we had purchased. She believed the simplest
and most immediate way to make a new place familiar,
and, above all else, comforting, was to have a nice well-
dressed bed when the sun set on your first unsettled day.
To this day, my preferred antidote to low spirits is to purchase new sheets, make my bed, take a bath, and tuck
myself into the crisp, cool sheets.

I didn't apply to any Historically Black Colleges and
Universities (HBCUs) where, contrary to conventional
bias, an unrivaled standard of education is afforded the
students in an environment unfamiliar to majority culture. My parents, both products of Howard University,
discouraged the HBCU route. They believed that my college experience should be a precursor to my future, one
of conquering the challenges of a majority-controlled
country. In the same vein, I was not to major in dance,
but in a subject that would provide a more likely path to
a sustainable job, security, and financial independence.

That academic immersion into a majority white environment between ages eleven and twenty-one steeled me and radicalized me for what was to come.

My parents took it a step further; I was to live in a traditional dormitory on campus, not at the hard-won Black student dorm across the street from the main gates of Vassar College, Kendrick House, referred to by our African American student community simply as "The House." Ours was the last entering class of freshmen to live there; it closed in 1975 following a decision by the New York Board of Regents that charged that Kendrick House was racially segregated. Although I didn't live in the house, a senior I soon began dating, did. Kendrick House was a refuge for Black students, whether we lived there or just hung out in that sacred gathering place for serious debate, organizing protests, self-defense lessons, all-night bid whist games, and parties; there was always familial drama, laughter, and tears.

At Vassar, I met and engaged with committed students who fought for and won many lasting and institutionalized changes on campus. These battles required the activism of the relatively limited enrollment of African American students on Vassar's campus and many others throughout our nation in the late 1960s and 1970s. In Vassar's case, many of these "demands," including for the College to honor the rights to equity and inclusion of its African American students, had been won as concessions made by the College during an historic 1969 "takeover" of Vassar's Main Building, where the heart of the college's communications systems resided. While the group comprised thirty-four young African American women from freshmen to seniors, they were icons to many of us who enrolled at Vassar after them. They altered the paradigm for us, opened the door a bit wider for a new demographic of inner-city Black students, secured Kendrick House, and institutionalized the Africana Studies program. All their

nine demands were won at the end of their meticulously planned takeover. They executed the only all-Black female student occupation of the time, and the *New York
Times* ran a front-page story with a photograph of one of
the group at a window. At a recent 50th year celebration of
Vassar's Africana Studies program, some of the members
of the takeover spoke about their memories of the event.
One paid tribute to the women who dressed in black at 3
a.m., fearful but resolute, and calmly took their positions
in the communication center, dismissed the switchboard
operator, nailed the doors shut with slabs of wood, and
made crystal clear to Vassar's then president Alan Simp-
son that they were committed to maintain control as long
as necessary. The activists prevailed in only three days.

Our Vassar family remains united in the struggle both
on campus and throughout the world. On many campuses across the country, we and others fought to op-
pose unjust domestic and global actions that were rampant in the 1960s and 1970s, including the Vietnam War,
apartheid in South Africa, the dismantling of colonialism
globally, the absence of diversity at institutions of higher
learning in admissions policies and practices, diversity
among faculty and trustees, concerns about discriminatory and retaliatory actions of classmates and professors
in the majority community against students of color,
and the beat goes on. We continue to need to do battle
much too often today, after decades of donning in pride
and protest our kente cloth-draped graduation gowns.
It is a tradition we alumni of that era have passed down
in an annual pre-graduation rite of passage ceremony
for African American graduating seniors at Vassar. It in-
volves the presentation of a traditional Ghanaian woven
kente cloth to be worn over the collar with cap and gown
and is considered by some recipients as more significant
than their traditional graduation wear. Further, the activists of yesteryear support our younger and current

47

From left: Yolanda Sabio '73, Sheila Wright '72, Dena Henderson Sewell '72, Beatrix Fields '72, Patricia James Jordan '72, Geneva Kellam '73, Claudia Thomas '71; *seated:* June Christmas '45–4 *(left)*, and Maybelle Taylor Bennett '70

students at an on-campus conference organized by the African American Alumni of Vassar College (known as Triple AVC) every three years. This conference provides current students with access to a powerful network of alumni throughout their time at Vassar and beyond.

Vassar alumni spanning more than seventy years come together at these conferences. We relish the opportunity to see and benefit from the wisdom of Dr. June Jackson Christmas, graduate of Vassar's class of 1945/44, one of the first recognized Black (several previous students "passed" for white) students. She attended Boston University Medical School, becoming a psychiatrist, founder of a community psychiatric program in Harlem—the Harlem Rehabilitation Center—and former New York City Commissioner of Public Health, among her many accomplishments. With her hallmark grace, she eloquently shared her story at our virtual conference in 2021, leaving the viewers on Zoom teary eyed with pride and reverence.

Dr. Claudia Thomas' book *God Spare Life,* describes her

journey of accomplishments and survival. Claudia, one of the thirty-four students who occupied Vassar's Main Building in protest, was the first African American female orthopedic surgeon in the US. Sister Vassar graduate Paula Williams Madison '74, journalist, former president and general manager of KNBC, making her the first African American woman to become general manager of a top news network, activist, and entrepreneur, traced her family's story in her book and documentary, *Finding Samuel Lowe: China, Jamaica, Harlem*. Her mission to discover and engage her maternal Chinese family debunks the many stereotypes and myths people of color shoulder. Reading their stories has inspired me to share mine, recognizing the rich history and value of the storytelling tradition passed down to us by our ancestors.

I strive to honor those fierce African American women at Vassar in the late 1960s, and later joined by Black men in the 1970s (after Vassar transitioned to a coeducational institution) who created and passed on a legacy of activism, determination, and achievement that many of us, as well as later generations would recognize and embrace. Indeed, it is a responsibility and an honor to be given the "privilege" of joining the ranks of the warrior tribe. Although there was frequent internecine warfare within the tribe, especially when the female members found themselves the victims of unacceptable polyamorous and entitled behavior of the newly admitted men. But, for the most part, the memories we treasured were the sense of community, our joyful passage from adolescence to adulthood, and the development of long-lasting and unbreakable bonds of friendship and support.

While my days at Vassar included the joys and pains of growing into adulthood, I never was far away from my parents' directives regarding my college studies. During the years I attended Vassar, 1973–1977, there was no dance major. Therefore, I had no opportunity to

Kendall Beane and Lauri at Vassar College Dance
Studio, circa 1972, *brochure courtesy of Vassar College*

defy my father's admonition. So, my greatest transgression involved taking most of the available dance classes, performing with Vassar Dance Theatre, choreographing, and expanding my training to embrace modern and contemporary dance. Here I was at college and trying to maintain the rigor to which I had grown accustomed at Jones-Haywood.

My first reaction to college life was the unfamiliar and initially disconcerting relationship with time. Never before in my very disciplined and heavily scheduled days did I have so many free hours. I vacillated between elation and fear. Without classes and study filling my entire day, every day, what was I to do? I discovered the Vassar experience was never boring nor was it predictable. It was instead action packed with drama and joy. I majored in Hispanic Studies, not a surprise, given my love of the Spanish language and its presence in my life since elementary school. My campus job was in the office of the language building, where I also continued to study German.

If there had been a "minor" at Vassar, Africana Studies

would have been mine. I loved my professors, our discussions, the authors to whom I was introduced, and the rich history about Africans and the Diaspora that I learned. Much like my comfort at Jones-Haywood with dance students who looked like me, or the refuge of Kendrick House, the Africana Studies Department was the only place on Vassar's campus where we African American students were in the majority, under the tutelage of brilliant professors of color. That sense of comfort was absent in my other academic classes. And, as always, in dance class, the movement and music never failed to transport me to that place of inner peace and comfort, no matter where or with whom I was.

Admittedly, the committed activists and revolutionaries were surprised and thrilled when Earth, Wind and Fire performed on our campus, as did the Dance Theatre of Harlem (DTH). It was at the Vassar master class taught by none other than Arthur Mitchell himself, that he recognized me and noted that I was a Jones-Haywood product whom he had taught on occasion and evaluated for a continuing Ford Foundation dance scholarship. He approached me in class at the barre and asked in a familiar and sweetly menacing tone, "What are you doing *here*?" I responded timidly that I was studying for my bachelor's degree. He invited me and another Vassar student, Myra Morris, who hailed from Poughkeepsie, to take classes at DTH during our winter school break. It was a dream come true to have a taste of the life of a professional dancer, with daily "company classes" taught by the famous Karel Shook, and prima ballerina Tannequil Le Clerc, one of several former wives of Balanchine, who taught from her wheelchair. Myra Morris, who had studied all her life at a local ballet school in Poughkeepsie, and I were roommates at International House in New York City, a reasonably priced boarding house for many aspiring young people. The schedule of multiple classes each day for several weeks was sweet torture. A friend from Jones-Haywood, who, like me, had gone away to college, left school to join the Alvin Ailey Dance Company that winter. I knew that I could not break my parents' hearts that way, so this was not a choice I could make; so, after winter break, back to Vassar I went to complete my sophomore year.

My Vassar experience, not unlike the experience of many others who count themselves lucky to have attended college at all, was seminal. I thrived in an environment of academic excellence and honed my activist character. My creative abilities grew and were allowed to flourish in both organized and spontaneous performance vehicles, many arranged by exceptionally talented singers, actors, dancers, directors, producers, and writers within our Vassar community.

I joined formal and informal groups including one studying Marxist Leninist Mao Tse Tung Thought (MLMTT). I can chuckle now about how "cool" my parents were on our drive home after my graduation. They had attended my graduation events, met my classmates, and accepted congratulations from their parents for my graduating with honors and being accepted into the ranks of Phi Beta Kappa. In the car ride home from Poughkeepsie, I was full of the spirit of accomplishment, but with nontraditional plans for my immediate future, after an incredible education at one of the country's elite "seven sister schools." Hitching a ride with us to DC was an African fellow graduate. On the road, I announced to my parents that I would be joining a collective of my MLMTT comrades to work on the assembly line at a factory in North Carolina. Although I could only see their eyes in the rearview mirror, I recall the astounded looks and facial expressions of my parents, and the disbelief on our guest passenger's face at the seemingly calm, neutral, and inquisitive reaction from my parents. A

Dad, Lauri, and Mom at Vassar graduation, 1977

few weeks later, when I'd had time to reflect on my college experience and consider my future options, my factory-bound comrades stopped at my house to pick me up on their journey south and I diplomatically demurred, my mother finally audibly exhaled. My paternal grandparents lived next to a shirt factory in Warrenton, North Carolina. Every time we drove to visit them and turned off the highway passing the shirt factory, my parents would turn to me in the back seat to ask if I wanted to be dropped off there.

At Vassar, the college having recently turned coed, I began a relationship with Ricky Roberts, a tall, smart, socially conscious man who was also an accomplished musician, and political science and Africana Studies major. We dated for ten years, through my Vassar years in Poughkeepsie and junior year semester in Spain, and while he was in grad school and law school in Vermont, Kenya, and New York City, as well as during my two diplomatic tours in the Dominican Republic and Mexico. Finally, with both of us back in Washington, we lived together for nine months. Previously, we were rarely in the same city, in the same country, or even on the same continent. Distance rarely enhances bonding in a romantic

Lauri and Ricky Roberts

relationship, particularly when the partners are in critical stages of growth, discovery, and self-awareness. We had genuine and strong feelings for each other, were compatible, and we both made efforts to accommodate each other's academic, professional, and social opportunities. But I feel that unmet expectations and a lack of emotional maturity complicated our chances to continue the stable and mutually gratifying relationship that we had initiated in my first indelible year at Vassar. Ironically, when we finally had the opportunity to eliminate the distance and live together, we discovered that too much time had clouded our path forward and the relationship finally ended.

It was through the relationship with Ricky, however, that I first heard accounts of the legendary women of the 1968 takeover at Vassar and was introduced to many of them. Through him and with him I developed my own friendships with many of those young men and women. With them, I engaged in activism, gained a true sense of community, embraced an extended African American family, honed my political consciousness, and became like them, a proud warrior.

The spring before I enrolled at Vassar in 1973, I traveled to Spain during Semana Santa (Holy Week) with Mom and a group of junior high school students. I lost my passport in Málaga and had to get a new one issued by the US Embassy in Madrid before our return date. A bit nervous and confused about finding the Embassy on my own, I asked Santiago, a bellboy at our hotel, Florida Norte, for guidance. He agreed to accompany me the next day to pick up my replacement passport. That day, we discovered that we were born in the same month, on the same day, and in the same year. We became pen pals and exchanged letters from then forward. We communicated only in Spanish, contributing to my fluency, as well as a priceless education about Spain's poets, novelists, and music. I treasured those letters and recently sent him a photograph of the rubber band-secured stacks I keep.

I returned to Madrid two years later in 1975 when I spent the first semester of my junior year at Vassar in Spain; my roommate Sandy Ramsey and I spent as little time as possible in the home of our host couple. They were paid to house and feed us, but while we saw them eating steak, we were given spaghetti and occasionally chicken. Upon returning to the house late at night, I would meet Sandy in the kitchen where I sometimes joined her as she peeled the flat "Maria" cookies from their cylindrical packages, spread butter on top, and ate them to quiet the hunger pangs before retreating to our bedroom. I reunited with Sandy and her husband at a Vassar reunion a few years ago and we reminisced about our memorable junior year in Madrid at the Instituto Internacional.

I was luckier than Sandy because after spending most of my evenings with Santiago Martinez and his friends, I often went to his home where we joined his parents for the customary late-night dinner in Madrid. His parents were always kind to me, but his father was not fond of Americans and questioned me often about my life in the US.

Approaching fifty years later, Santiago still rescues me.

From left: Sara Martinez, Lauri, Santiago, and María Izquierdo

He always "gets me" and knows what is best, sometimes before I do. We have a connection and feel that we are "twins separated at birth." I met Santiago in Madrid, when we were seventeen. He and his wife María entrusted my husband Fernando and me with their beloved only child, Sara, and her friend Susana one summer when Sara was sixteen. When my daughter Briana and I first visited Santi and his family, in Santibáñez, an endearing hamlet in Spain, surrounded by fields of giant sunflowers, where his wife María grew up, Briana was sixteen.

In Santibáñez, located in the province of Salamanca and the region of Leon, visitors parked their cars after arriving and never needed them until they departed or decided to venture to another town. The older people gathered to play cards outside in the evenings before supper. The aroma of freshly baked bread and homemade desserts filled the air when they arrived in a truck, which the town's women surrounded to carefully select what they needed until the truck would make its next run. Fresh fruits and vegetables were always available in the town's tiny shops, and also from any neighbor's garden. Aromas of grilling fish and other local dishes

Margaret Tynes von Klier,
courtesy of Richard Roberts

filled the evening air when the streets emptied, and everyone returned to the family table for the traditionally late evening Spanish supper, only to reemerge after the meal to congregate at the local bar for conversation and a caña (glass of beer) or a drink. The children played in the streets until midnight.

During my junior year semester break in Madrid, I visited Italy to spend a week with renowned opera singer Margaret Tynes, my then boyfriend Ricky's aunt, his mother's sister. I have had an incomparable and lasting relationship with Aunt Margaret, a stunning opera singer from North Carolina, who, like many talented African American artists, was better accepted and afforded performance opportunities in Canada and throughout Europe than in her own country. She gained international acclaim when Giancarlo Menotti engaged her for eight sensational performances of *Salome* at the Spoleto "Festival of Two Worlds" conducted by Thomas Schippers and directed by the renowned Italian stage and film producer, Luchino Visonti. Since that triumph, she appeared with the leading opera companies of Europe and the US: the Metropolitan Opera, the Vienna Staatsoper, the Operas of Prague, Budapest, and Bologna, and the Barcelona Liceo.

Margaret's pre-opera professional experience began in the field of popular music with *Finian's Rainbow* on Broadway, in Harry Belafonte's *Sing, Man, Sing*, Duke Ellington's recording of *A Drum Is a Woman*, and Ed Sullivan's State Department-sponsored tour of the Soviet Union. Along her journeys through Europe, she also met and married Czech-born architect and prominent designer, Baron Hans von Klier. They taught me many life lessons and exposed me to a world I had never imagined.

I first met Aunt Margaret in New York where she stayed with her renowned voice coach, Lola Hayes, in a fabulous apartment on Fifth Avenue. It was through Aunt Margaret that I finally met my cousin from Warrenton, North Carolina, opera singer and professor, Hilda Harris. Hilda is from my father's side of the family, and is related to me through our mutual relative, Bishop Brevard Harris. Aunt Margaret knew her well because Ms. Hayes had also been Cousin Hilda's voice coach.

Mezzo-soprano Hilda Harris, formerly a leading artist of the Metropolitan Opera, has performed throughout the United States and Europe. She established herself as a singing actress and has earned critical acclaim in opera, on the concert stage, and in recital. At the Metropolitan Opera, she made her debut as the Student in *Lulu*, and sang "Cherubino" (*Le Nozze di Figaro*), The Child (*L'Enfant et les Sortilèges*), Siebel (*Faust*), Stephano (*Romeo et Juliette*), Hansel (*Hansel & Gretel*), and Sesto (*Giulio Cesare*). She also has sung such roles as Carmen in St. Gallen, in Brussels, and in Budapest. She has taught at the Manhattan School of Music, Howard University, and Sarah Lawrence College.

I spent many unforgettable hours with Aunt Margaret with her nephew Ricky and his sister, my good friend Adrienne, in the spectacular Manhattan apartment where she stayed on her visits to New York; Aunt Margaret, Adrienne (who then lived in New York City), and I often would retreat to her spacious bedroom where the three of us giggled and gossiped like schoolgirls.

I was giddy with excitement when I was invited to Aunt Margaret and Uncle Hans' home in Milan, Italy for a week's visit in 1975 during a school break from my studies in Madrid. What an adventure I had, traveling by train from Madrid to Milan in the "cattle car," a small compartment for six people, with three facing another three on hard, wooden, straight-back benches, with our knees almost touching the person across from us. Changing trains somewhere in France was a scene from a movie, as one of my compartment mates and I ran from one train to the next, jumping onto the moving train for our onward journey—thankfully, he carried my bag, as we almost missed our connection.

I arrived at the cavernous Milan train station, looked around as I listened to all of the announcements in Italian and hoped to lock eyes with someone familiar, when a very handsome, elegant, and tall man strode toward me, and smiling, spoke my name the way my Spanish friends and Aunt Marg pronounced it, "Lowri" (rhyming with dowry). Good thing I didn't know how the "au" was pronounced in romance languages when I was a child and thought the lyrics of the popular Italian song "Volare" was actually "Oh Lauri" as I skipped along singing, proud to know that my name was memorialized in a world-famous song!

Uncle Hans greeted me with kisses on each cheek (I think it was two in Italy, as I soon learned how many kisses were the custom throughout the world). We had an espresso at the station and proceeded home to their beautifully appointed apartment. I, in my grungy clothing after the many hours of travel, was greeted warmly by Aunt Margaret at the door and immediately told,

"Just drop your coat and shoes right there and follow me to the nice hot bath I have waiting for you." She, of course, transformed me into a young woman she could show off to all her friends. During my stay, I accompanied Aunt Margaret and Uncle Hans to restaurants, receptions, and fabulous events in Italy's fashion capital. They took me to Turin one day where Aunt Margaret was busy rehearsing. During my stay, Uncle Hans generously took me to Florence, Venice, and to the Vatican. I tried to contain my delight and conduct myself with sophistication and aplomb. When the week ended much too quickly and I prepared for the long train ride back to Madrid, I was so grateful to Aunt Margaret and Uncle Hans when they surprised me with a plane ticket back to Madrid to continue my studies. My thoughts were in the clouds that week and long after I boarded the plane.

After Uncle Hans' death, Aunt Margaret returned to the US in the mid 1990s and moved into a retirement community near Washington, DC, to be close to her family. On one occasion, I surprised her by taking her to an event where Harry Belafonte was the guest speaker. Forever the diva, she was thrilled when I brought him over to greet her, and they chatted for a few moments about old times. When Fernando and I were still married, we hosted a reception for Aunt Margaret at our home, to her delight. She turned one hundred years old on September 11, 2018. As she has lost her sight and memory, I have preferred to remember her as she was, well into her golden years: the vibrant woman who talked to me about everything, shared stories about her fairy-tale life, and taught me so much about living in a magical world. Having Aunt Margaret in my life contributed to my confidence and self-awareness, which has helped to inform many successful periods in my life.

My junior year in Madrid was my first of several periods as an expatriate living outside the US. Not only did I live in Spain at the moment of longtime dictator Francisco Franco's death on November 20, 1975, but I also witnessed the end of a painful era in Spain and the launch of an uncertain future. Not knowing that he died that day, I emerged from the Ruben Dario subway station and noted the lack of activity on the streets. I walked the short blocks to the Instituto Internacional where the Vassar-Wesleyan program held classes, only to be astounded to see a simple sign on the locked door that said, "Generalissimo Francisco Franco died. No classes today." I have returned to Spain many times since then, finding familiarity and comfort born of a time when I was young and impressionable.

I had first traveled to Spain on an ordinary passport, but soon after graduating from Vassar, I would travel to several countries on my diplomatic passport, as my transition to the Foreign Service came just two years after my junior semester abroad. I would become a rare "threefer" diplomat—exceptionally young, African American, and female.

CHAPTER FOUR

Ballet Santo Domingo

M y first diplomatic assignment was shared with an unprecedented, uncharacteristically diverse group of first-tour junior officers in Santo Domingo, Dominican Republic, in 1978. We easily could have been featured on the avant-garde billboards and television commercials featuring multiracial faces promoting the "United Colors of Benetton." All my State Department junior officer colleagues had to "do time" on the abhorred visa line, deciding the fate of hopeful Dominican travelers to the United States who either hated or idolized them, depending upon whether they were granted their visa.

On the other hand, I experienced the few advantages of being in a branch of the Foreign Service other than the predominant State Department corps. Few Americans even know that several other agencies contribute diplomats to our Foreign Service. I was honored to serve my country first as a career Foreign Service Officer supporting cultural and educational programs at the now defunct US Information Agency (USIA) (now subsumed into the "public diplomacy" section of the State Department) and later as a political appointee heading a Foreign Service agency, the Foreign Commercial Service (FCS), a rare if not unique career trajectory.

I had an exceptional training ground as an awardee of a Federal Junior Fellowship beginning the summer after graduation from high school, thanks to my father's theater friend, Helen Murphy, who worked at USIA. Coincidentally, I had been her daughter Nellie's ballet instructor at Jones-Haywood, when I taught the four- to five-year-old class at Jones-Haywood throughout my teenage years. I was a Federal Junior Fellow during summers and college breaks from 1973 to 1975 at the Department of Health and Welfare, Food and Drug Administration, Procurement Branch, in Rockville, Maryland. I was taught by a warm and welcoming team of civil servants to complete handwritten requisition forms according to meticulous protocols for FDA supplies and, sometimes mice (for experimentation, I assumed). I delighted and thrived among my colleagues, primarily middle-aged, who appreciated my energy, enthusiasm, and innocent fascination with what they had grown to consider mundane.

In the summer of 1975 after my sophomore year at Vassar, I had cut my teeth at FDA, maintained my high school trend of excellent academic achievement at Vassar, and focused my academic interests largely on things global, I was given a bittersweet farewell party by supportive Procurement Office colleagues. I was reassigned from 1975 to 1977 to the USIA Office of Public Affairs in Washington, DC, with headquarters on Pennsylvania Avenue a stone's throw from the White House at 1600 Pennsylvania Avenue. I reported to USIA Public Affairs, led by a strong, imposing yet attentive and kind woman, Ruth Walters. The office was located at the Voice of America (VOA), on Independence Avenue SW, with the Capitol and the Mall so close for an occasional lunchtime stroll. My duties included conducting tours of the Voice of America exhibit and studios in English and Spanish; identifying, splicing, and transcribing breaking news stories for the producers and broadcasters in VOA's Spanish language service; and responding to phone inquiries in the Public Affairs Office of USIA. Helen Murphy, my first career mentor, encouraged me to pursue a diplomatic career.

In 1977, after graduating from Vassar and completing my four-year US government fellowship, I became a full-time employee at USIA. At the same time, with advice from USIA colleagues, friends and family, I prepared diligently for the rigorous last rites of "hazing"—including an oral exam, an essay, and an "in basket" test to become a diplomat. The oral exam was administered and assessed by a panel of Foreign Service Officers, who could ask any range of questions, making it difficult to narrow preparation. Eric Holder, a friend then living in DC and working at his first Department of Justice job, gave me a useful pearl of advice, "Read *The Economist* magazine cover to cover." The "in basket" test comprised receiving a paper filled "in box" of memos and documents for sorting, prioritizing, and responding; the test assesses organization, judgement, ability to delegate, and teamwork. It is timed. I wrote essays in response to several questions for that portion. All I can say is I was sweatin' during those few hours, more than the puddles of perspiration circling my body at the barre during a tough warm-up in the unairconditioned ballet studio. I passed at age twenty-one, making me among the youngest (average age was thirty-plus) junior officers of my time.

Meanwhile, my day job was working in USIA's Foreign Service personnel office. During that time, I met Ethel Payne, an African American trailblazer in journalism who was serving on a board considering promotions for Foreign Service Officers. I was pleased and surprised to see her on the review panel in 1977. Upon meeting me and learning my background, we remained in contact for many years, and she was always generous with her advice and life lessons. After a few months, I worked for Jeff Liteman on plans for my own Junior Officer Training (JOT) program. I quickly passed my Spanish language exam (immediately removing me from language probation) and successfully completed my US-based JOT program. In early 1978, I was the first or second in my class to be deployed to my first tour, my first choice of the three selections, the Dominican Republic. I had celebrated my twenty-second birthday that previous fall.

Arriving at the Santo Domingo airport, I was welcomed by the Public Affairs Officer (PAO) who headed the USIA team. Holly Mack Bell, who was dressed in a blue and white seersucker suit, was accompanied by his wife, Clara Bell, who arrived in pristine white gloves, a dress and panty hose. It was June, and in the sweltering heat, there they were, greeting me formally with deep Southern drawls. The moment was reminiscent of a scene from the movie *Gone with the Wind*, and I was the surprise arrival at the Big House. As they extended their hands to shake mine, I hesitated, wondering whether I should shake hands or simply curtsy. Although extremely proper and formal in his demeanor, Holly Bell proved to be a warm and considerate head of section. My immediate boss, Tim Randall, was his opposite, and he made the job fun every day, with his wonderful sense of humor and easygoing management style. My Dominican colleagues were all characters, with each more friendly and helpful than the last. Among them were Franklin Polanco, an institution in the Embassy and city and his lovely wife Patria, and a woman who became my dear friend and guide, Floriana Piña.

While my colleagues labored on the visa line, my rookie tour in Santo Domingo included guiding New York Philharmonic conductor Zubin Mehta and his wife around the island when the orchestra visited Santo Domingo as part of USIA's cultural exchange program. I would welcome visiting US officials and introduce them to local art, artists, and museums. I also designed and supported initiatives for visiting American students on academic exchange programs. I was a first-tour Foreign Service Officer engaged in cultural diplomacy which made my later role in commercial diplomacy that much easier.

My career Foreign Service experience in Santo Domingo prepared me well for my duties twenty-five years later as Assistant Secretary and Director General (DG) of the Foreign Commercial Service position at the Commerce. My service in Santo Domingo enabled me to understand the challenges that are associated with being a diplomat serving our country abroad. Perhaps naively all those years later, I expected those credentials would serve me well, engendering credibility and respect from my new employees. I should have anticipated that would not always be the case with many of the Foreign Commercial Officers and some of the political appointees under my charge. I'm sure the resistance to accepting my authority, despite my broad experience, credentials and earlier experience in the Foreign Service, stemmed from many factors: my embattled confirmation by the US Senate required for the position for which I was nominated by the president; my long friendship with Secretary Brown; and simply the reality of being a young Black woman leading an entitled, predominantly white male civil service and Foreign Service staff. I have great respect for our country's, diplomats who are often undervalued, misunderstood, and often stereotyped. They seldom are honored for their service, the sacrifices that they make, or for their contributions to the position of the US in the world. They often live at risk, working long hours, may be separated from family, and must uproot themselves, leaving one assignment to create new homes for themselves and their families in disparate ports of call. The Foreign Service achieved far wider racial diversity in the 1970s and 1980s when we were Junior Officer Trainees in Santo Domingo compared to today. The sad but still prevailing view that minority recruits to the service enter at a disadvantage because they are not "pale, Yale, and male" was rendered a myth, due to the high number of those from our group who rose to the senior foreign service as Ambassadors and Assistant Secretaries. Today, the diversity statistics for the Foreign Service are abysmal for minorities and only slightly better for women. I welcome the programs over the last twenty years to identify and support entry of diverse candidates from college and graduate schools to the Foreign Service. However, these programs have not been as successful as anticipated for these new officers who face a foreign service entrenched in traditional practices and ironically, although effective in dealing with other global cultures, is lacking in cultural competence and acceptance of their own diverse American colleagues.

I applaud, nonetheless, efforts to better support young and mid-career officers who represent the diversity of America, to better communicate what diplomats do, and to provide examples of their accomplishments to the general public, through podcasts, reports and speaking opportunities. I especially appreciate and applaud the work of the Association for Diplomatic Studies and Training (ADST). They produce oral histories of Foreign Service Officers, used for research by students and professionals and stored at the Library of Congress. I am proud to continue my service and commitment to our foreign service as a board member of this valuable organization.

I met many supportive role models and developed lifelong mentors at USIA during those formative years, including, in addition to Helen, John Gravely. He joined the Foreign Service in 1968, but was a civil servant at USIA when we met, committed to minority recruitment and college fellowships for youths interested in Foreign

Service careers. He was instrumental to the establish-ment of the Pickering Program, designed to recruit can-didates of color to the Foreign Service. Gravely later be-came a pastor at Church of the Redeemer in DC and was as dedicated to the disenfranchised of that city as he had been committed to change, civil rights, and social justice during his twenty-seven-year government career.

Imagine the thrill of meeting George Haley, the broth-er of *Roots* author Alex Haley, working at USIA. Meeting George Haley made me recall the excitement of hav-ing watched the TV series at Vassar, huddled in Shelley Hayes' room in Lathrop House. Shelley was one of the few I knew in our Lathrop House dormitory who had a television in her room! The book and TV series were seminal for African Americans, young and old, marking the first time our uncensored history had been portrayed on prime-time television, tracing not just one Black fam-ily's ancestry, but creating for the first time broad public consumption of the unfiltered, harsh realities of slavery.

Ships of enslaved Africans had also reached the shores of countries in the Caribbean, including the Dominican Republic, where the mixture of Spanish, Indigenous, and African genes created a population with complex-ions ranging from white to many shades of brown. There was also a variety of hair textures and facial features, reflecting the characteristics of the colonizers, the Af-ricans, and Indians. While in the Dominican Republic, I discovered that however multicolored that country was, the customary preference for lighter skin was as strong there as in the US.

I learned that former Dominican president Trujillo had powdered his face to appear fairer skinned. It was also during his leadership in 1937 that the famous Parsley massacre of Haitians occurred. Haitians had been brought across the land border to become chattel in the DR, and they soon became the backbone of the Dominican sugar industry. I realized how deeply disturbing it was for me to see Haitians in this condition, given that Haiti had so early won its independence from French colonizers. During an ugly period in the history of the two countries, predominantly darker-skinned Haitian workers in the DR were systematically targeted and killed. The Dominican tormentors found one way of distinguishing Haitians from Dominicans, that involved asking a suspected Haitian to pronounce the word "perejil" (parsley). Apparently, if spoken from the lips of a Haitian native French or Kreyol speaker, the slight rolling of the "r" sound would prove difficult and thereby identify the person as Haitian. How demoralizing it is that the historical antipathy between the DR and Haiti continues even today, even though they share one small island; Hispaniola is unevenly divided with Haiti occupying the lesser one-third of the island's landmass, and the DR the larger two-thirds.

Peter Romero, of Puerto Rican descent, and I share laughs about our experience of race identification in Dominican society. We were made aware of it when we went to get the required carnet (identification card). I was listed as "Indio/a," (referring to the Indigenous people of the country), considered a socially more acceptable classification for nonwhite people. I protested this classification with the authorities, explaining that I was indeed "Negra" (Black) to no avail. They insisted as if I were asking to be called the N-word saying, "Oh noooo señora, usted no es negra, usted es india." The reality is that the Indigenous Indians who originally inhabited the country were nonexistent by then, extinct through the effects of colonization and mixing of the races with enslaved Africans and Europeans.

It was my impression that the mixture of races and ethnicities had resulted in a country of very attractive people. I returned to the DR in the mid-1980s on vacation with my then boyfriend, Lon Walls. As we traveled through the Dominican countryside by car, I thought he would get whiplash from constantly snapping his head around to gawk at the sight of one woman more stunning than the last. Thank goodness I was the one driving and was more amused than jealous! In fact, two Foreign Service Officers in our first diplomatic tour group each married Dominican women.

I was thrilled to soon discover a ballet school and company, Ballet Santo Domingo, operating under the direction of Irmgard Despradel. Given my cultural portfolio at the Embassy, there was no objection to my moonlighting as a dancer, once again. I was welcomed by my new dance company and cast to participate in many performances. Here I was on my first venture living on my own, alone as a young professional in a foreign country, and ballet was again providing me with a familiar and grounded feeling. At Ballet Santo Domingo, I performed in *Coppélia,* other classical ballets, and contemporary works. Armando Villamil, a Panamanian resident dancer/choreographer, created contemporary choreography that depicted stories of historical and social significance. I was honored to perform with him in the role of the aggrieved mixed race "mulata" in one piece choreographed to music by Cuban composer, Ernesto Lecuona. In line with my day job responsibility in cultural affairs, I arranged for my friend and ballerina Sandra Fortune-Green to be invited as a visiting guest teacher and artist at Ballet Santo Domingo—a meaningful and fun reunion for us and a unique experience for the ballet company to have a world-acclaimed American ballerina of color among them.

In 1979, Irmgard, Armando, and I traveled to Panama to explore opportunities for Ballet Santo Domingo to perform there. I had no idea I would meet the famous de facto leader of the country, Omar Torrijos, who took power in a coup d'état and was known as the Leader of the Panamanian Revolution. He also had negotiated with

Lauri dancing *Coppélia* with
Ballet Santo Domingo,
Dominican Republic

Lauri and Armando Villamil

President Jimmy Carter what became known as the Panama Canal Treaty. Armando picked us up one day in a red SUV, and we headed outside the city to the beach town of Farallon to a lovely home on the Pacific Ocean. There were a few aides and security scattered around the property. We were escorted in to see a somewhat-imposing man wearing a guayabera (a traditional shirt with a collar and buttons down front, preferred to dress shirts and suit jackets in warm Caribbean and Central American countries), who greeted us warmly and welcomed Armando like a long-lost brother. Irmgard and I were introduced to "El Jefe," General Torrijos, as Armando's friends and dancers in Santo Domingo. That I was an American and a diplomat was never mentioned by anyone during that entire afternoon.

We had lunch, and the conversation moved among many topics. My accent in Spanish never identified me as an American, and my fluency in the language has often led native speakers to consistently question me about my Latina roots. Since I was assumed to be Dominican or Panamanian, I had no reason to explain my language skills, but El Jefe's interest in me was immediately apparent. As the afternoon progressed and he tried to become increasingly more familiar with me, my discomfort grew. He was a tough negotiator who expressed both positive and negative impressions about the US; he both loved and hated it. It was clear that on that day he was playing to the "hate" constituency. It began at lunch when he commanded me to sit near him at the table, "siéntate aquí, mi prieta" (in this context, an endearing term meaning my Black woman). I made it through lunch talking little and listening as he excoriated Americans. Suddenly he rose from his seat and told the group we were going for a ride. I was looking forward to a tour of the town or a trip to the beautiful beach. Instead, we pulled up to a small aircraft and were escorted to our seats. After a relatively short and uneventful flight, we landed on a makeshift dirt runway and were greeted by a crowd of admiring townspeople. Like the Pied Piper, we were surrounded by the crowd, and led on a jubilant, meandering walk to a modest home in the town. Surrounded by an adoring group of men, El Jefe took a seat in the backyard at a table where glasses and bottles of whiskey were arrayed. He instructed Irmgard and me to sit in chairs a few feet behind the table, but well within earshot of the lively conversation, where he regaled his

General Omar Torrijos with crowd

admiring audience with boastful stories about his nego-
tiations with the difficult Americans.

After much consumption of alcohol, as the sun descended, we all—El Jefe, and his merry band of supporters—made our way back to the small aircraft. As we
headed into the plane, we could see that every car in the
town had lined up on either side of the dirt runway with
headlights blazing to illuminate the airplane's path for
takeoff. El Jefe staggered to his seat and immediately fell
asleep. I was wide-eyed and in awe that the tiny plane
managed to successfully ascend and land in Panama City.
Armando must have convinced the pilot and security to
allow us to be dropped off there, and then to take El Jefe
back to Farallon. As we disembarked from that aircraft,
leaving Torrijos snoring, I stopped holding my breath and
finally exhaled. Upon arriving at our hotel, Irmgard and I
looked at each other in relief and amazement. Less than
two years later, in 1981, El Jefe—the man who was able to
finally wrest control of the Panama Canal from the United
States; the man who loved life and lived large; the man
who was adored by his countrymen—would become one
of seven killed in a Panamanian Air Force Twin Otter plane
that crashed into the side of Panama's Marta Hill. I will always wonder if that plane was the same one we boarded
on that memorable afternoon and evening in Panama all
those many years ago when El Jefe thought I was Latina
and called me "mi prieta."

As I transitioned to my new life in the Foreign Service, my dancing and my new colleagues created comfort. Looking back, I now realize how much easier being a
diplomat was then, compared to the post-9/11 overseas
tours of more recent US diplomats. In the early 1980s,
we didn't have the security concerns and limitations on
our movements that are consequences of that turning
point in US history. Our group, often with Dominican colleagues and friends, traveled freely on weekends savor-

ing the food, experiencing the culture, and exploring the pristine expanses of crystal-clear beaches. So spoiled am I by this early life, that I can't now swim in water—I can't see through to the surface below.

I am forever grateful to my Cuban American colleague and friend, Lino Gutierrez, for the body of knowledge he shared about Cuban music, his life story as an immigrant, his incredible command over historical facts, and the adventures he often led. Our junior officer core group traveled extensively throughout the beautiful island country to remote and untouched places. On one occasion, Peter Romero, a member of that esteemed group, and I organized and accompanied our Ambassador, Robert Yost, and his wife to parts of the country they didn't yet know—Las Terrenas and Samaná—where an enclave of Black, English-speaking, protestant Dominicans lived. So exceptionally beautiful were those Northern shores of the Caribbean Sea and Eastern peninsula that the Yosts built a home in that area where I visited them many years later.

I particularly enjoyed the education and exposure I gained from my rotation in the Embassy's political section, where even though I was a USIA officer, I was afforded the opportunity to walk in the shoes of an incoming State Department officer selected to specialize in political affairs. I met and connected immediately with the administrative undersecretary of the presidency, Sonia Guzman, the daughter of the Dominican Republic President Antonio Guzman Fernandez. President Guzman had been a wealthy businessman and was credited with winning the election that ushered in the first peaceful transfer of power in the country. The Carter administration, and therefore the Embassy, supported that transition, and I learned firsthand about the fascinating events during that election from Lino, who was working with the master political attaché, John King. After President

Guzman had weathered many transition challenges and a devastating hurricane, just a month before his presidential term ended in 1982, Guzman shot himself in the head and was found dead in his office. Sonia Guzman is now the Dominican Ambassador to the United States.

I recall that during our tour, the movie *Saturday Night Fever* starring John Travolta had become immensely popular. The rhythm of the hit song, Travolta's famous swagger, and his dance moves reverberate in my head. These are coupled with flashbacks of many nights spent with my colleagues, dancing until we dropped at our favorite Santo Domingo disco. Mirta Alvarez, another Cuban American junior officer, was the leader of the John Travolta fan club in addition to winning the prize for the best housing and furniture. Her penthouse apartment and Embassy-issued furniture seemed to be in a different class than that of the rest of us, although our housing and lifestyle left us no reason to complain. We all worked hard at our jobs and played hard together.

Our group of first-tour officers in Santo Domingo coined the name "El Grupito" for ourselves. Most from our first tour of duty (Lino Gutierrez, Dennise Mathieu, Marcie Ries, Charlie Ries, Peter Romero, and Mike Senko) became career ambassadors serving our country with distinction in far-flung world capitals where my work and vacations made me a frequent houseguest. I hold the record in the group for having visited our sister officer, Deborah McCarthy, in every post to which she was assigned, including when she was Ambassador to Lithuania, through good times and bad. Ruth Romero, my colleague Pete Romero's wife, a highly accomplished lawyer, activist, mother, and grandmother, has been there for us all of us in El Grupito, and has led by example, remaining a beloved icon of our group, even as she wades through her recent health challenges.

While we "originals" share a special bond, we have

El Grupito, *photographer Mike Senko*

embraced in our family a few others, including officers who succeeded us, as well as our spouses, children, and now grandchildren. We, and our children, have grown up together as we are inextricably connected through the cold periods and the fires of our lives. We share our blessings and calamities, providing support and advice, whether wanted or unwanted. Because many of us are now retired and engaged in fulfilling second chapters, we are even more likely to partake in playful sibling rivalries in person.

I know that our collegial bond helped us through the professional and personal challenges in our diplomatic career ascent and many other private and public sector jobs. But never during our hard-won climb to the top did we quite recapture the atmosphere of acceptance, equity, and inclusion that we enjoyed in Santo Domingo. I treasure the memories of those days when I easily lived and embraced a multicultural environment, met lifelong friends, and achieved a viable combination of profession and passion. It was among the most rewarding periods of my life.

There were few African American women in the US Foreign Service in the 1970s and early 1980s. After the DR, my onward assignment was to Mexico City, a much larger Embassy, city, and country, which was more impersonal; it was a huge adjustment from the joys of my life in Santo Domingo. At that larger post, I did meet other officers and staff of color and developed a few lasting friendships. One of my colleagues at the Embassy was Dr. Yolanda Robinson, a dynamic Cuban American from California who shared with me her exquisite tastes in interior design, food, and wine, and her fun-loving personality. Yolanda and I, along with Californian David Kurakane, a Japanese American, formed a unique and rare trio in Mexico in the early 1980s. One Friday evening, after we had enjoyed several tequila shots, we met at the Mexico City Airport with our weekend beach gear packed for an adventure. The three of us stood fixated on the noisy rotating departure board contemplating which of the planes we might board to one of the country's many beautiful beaches. We opted for Acapulco, easily bought our tickets for the short flight, and upon landing headed for the Princess Hotel. It was right on the beach in Acapulco and built in the shape of a pyramid. We didn't have a reservation and the hotel was a popular tourist destination. Nevertheless, traveling with Yolanda was always an adventure. She was an expert at charming and convinced the unsuspecting hotel desk staff that there must have been a mistake if they couldn't find our reservation. Her antics always resulted in getting us checked in to the most spacious and fabulous room in the hotel.

Yolanda and I missed few places or cultural events in Mexico. On other adventures, we followed local traditional celebrations in the city of Morelia on Día de los Muertos (All Saints Day) on the first of November. This is an especially important day in Mexico, and a few other Latin American cultures. We joined the townspeople on a small boat to the shore of a cemetery where families placed food on the graves of their loved ones. We drove to the deserted beaches of Oaxaca where we sat on the sand at sunset, drinking the champagne we kept chilled in the cooler we carried in the trunk of the car.

While I missed the flavor of Santo Domingo and the

friends who had been reassigned to countries far and wide, I enjoyed my new circle of colleagues and friends, including my staff of twelve men and one woman. My senior staff assistant was a fifty-something man named Enrique Esteinou, who had been at the Embassy for many years and who was very skeptical of me, a twenty-four-year-old Black woman, who had been assigned as his new boss. Needless to say, we became great colleagues and friends over my two-year tour. I gained the confidence of my staff by listening, learning, and respecting them, and it didn't hurt that I was fluent in their language. I expressed interest in their families, supported opportunities for their advancement, assigned them interesting projects in which to participate, and defended them when needed from unreasonable work demands and deadlines, a fairly frequent occurrence in our world of print and broadcast media responsibilities in the Public Afairs Division of the US Embassy, Mexico City. I not only coordinated placement of my old stomping ground, VOA radio programs in Mexico, but had several opportunities to facilitate and accompany Mexican television crews producing documentaries on US-Mexico issues most of which at the time were related to the border. I became quite familiar with the US-Mexico border towns and concerns during those years.

Today, the refugee and immigration crises has received a level of attention that has eclipsed all other pressing issues, and there seems limited hope of comprehensive solutions in a world with increasing political and economic crises. Unfortunately, the conditions in the countries to our south have generated increased numbers of economic and political migrants, and our nation has responded with too many ineffective remedies rooted in fear, ignorance, and racism.

During my two-year tour, our part of the Embassy remained stable with normal rotations of the career Foreign Service Officers: Public Affairs Officer Stanley Zuck-

Lauri and United States Ambassador to
Mexico John Gavin

erman, a tandem Deputy Warren Obluck and his wife
Carol Ludwig, Press Attaché Larry Ikels, Cultural Affairs
Officer Diane Conway, Barbara Moore, and Yolanda and
David. Intervening in that relative stability during my
two-year tour was a parade of ambassadorial political
appointees, including former Wisconsin governor Pat-
rick Lucey; the first Mexican American Ambassador Ju-
lian Nava, who was received poorly by the Mexican government; and Hollywood actor, John Gavin.

I had seen very few African American women during
my extensive travels in Mexico, so, at the tender age of
twenty-five, I was not familiar with the story of the won-
derfully warm, understated, middle-aged Black woman
who introduced herself to me simply as Betty. I can't
remember where I first met her. Perhaps on one of my
trips to Cuernavaca where she lived, or at the restaurant,
Las Mañanitas, named after the Mexican birthday song,
located about an hour's drive north of Mexico City. The
restaurant was set in a luscious, perfectly manicured
and fragrant garden replete with exotic birds. Its elegance, with arrays of blooming bushes, trees, and flowers, and the sculpture garden, with the work of Mexico's

most famous sculptors, provided a feast for the eyes. The food was equally exquisite.

Elizabeth Catlett was a graphic artist and sculptor who invited me into her gracious home, studio, and family. On several Sundays, I escaped the busy D.F. (Distrito Federal) of Mexico City and drove alone to visit her in my black turbo engine Mustang with the sunroof fully open, allowing the breeze and the afternoon's sunlight to kiss my face.

Elizabeth (Betty) was from my native Washington, DC, and like my parents, had attended Howard University. Born in 1915, she had traveled to Mexico City in 1946 to work at the Taller de Gráfica Popular (TGP), an artists' collective, with her then husband, the revered African American artist Charles White. The TGP was pivotal to her understanding of "mestizaje," a blend of Spanish, Indigenous, and African antecedents in Mexico, which had similarities to the African American experience depicted in her famous works. With Lois Jones, artist and teacher who lived in the 1930s and 1940s in exile in Paris where her work gained praise, Elizabeth Catlett helped to create what was coined by Freida High Tesfagiorgis as "Afrofemcentrist."

Her prints are more widely known because of her twenty years with the TGP. In 1950, she shifted primarily to sculpture, which I saw in her Cuernavaca studio at her home. Like many activists of the time, the US House Un-American Activities Committee investigated Elizabeth during the 1950s; in 1962 she acquired Mexican citizenship. When I met her, she lived a quiet life with her second husband, Mexican painter and muralist Francisco Mora, who had been a student of Diego Rivera.

When I have seen Catlett's famous works in more recent years, I realize I had been in the presence of greatness and had no idea. At the time I knew her, I doubt that she had met many young African American diplomats, so I am honored that our paths crossed, and that she opened her home to me. In retrospect, I think she hoped that I might be a candidate for the affections of her son, David, a quiet young artist who today is quite accomplished, as are his siblings and Elizabeth's grandchildren.

Other highlights of my tour in Mexico were hosting a reception for visiting Alvin Ailey dancers at my home in the neighborhood of Las Lomas de Chapultepec, where the US Ambassador's residence is also located. My apartment was in an old two-story building that had started life as a unique art deco house with a heavy oval brass and glass-paned door that oddly locked at the bottom. It had a cathedral ceiling in the large dining area and a fireplace. I often sprawled on the rug in front of the fireplace both for warmth and to read, think, or listen to music. It was my favorite spot in the house. I also had an expansive patio in the front of the house over the two-car garage that I shared with my Mexican neighbor, also a single woman. In it I parked my precious Mustang, my first new car, which my parents drove from Washington, DC, to deliver to me on a visit soon after my arrival. I borrowed the reel-to-reel projector from the Embassy and set up a "theater" in my garage, so I could show the ballet students from down the street, where I sometimes taught ballet, a film about the Dance Theatre of Harlem (DTH). One of those students became a professional dancer, moved to New York City, and danced with DTH for many years.

One day, I encountered Pamela Anderson, a Black woman from Chicago, walking on a street near the Embassy, who was assigned to Mexico City for the Bank of Chicago. She became a good friend and together we formed a trio with Vondelia Truell, another African American Foreign Service colleague at the Embassy. The three of us got together to listen to Motown, reminisce about life back home, and gossip about popular stars, movies, books, and world developments. We just relaxed together and didn't have to "code switch," change our pronunciation, and cadence to standard English. We all understood our cultural references, slang, and humor. Being together was an escape from the predominantly white power structure at our jobs, in a country of culturally diverse Mexicans (Indigenous and Spanish, with some Africans in coastal towns) who often stared at us in public places. We were not part of the white American power elite or the Mexican culture, so we sought refuge among ourselves. Pam and I, after sharing that time in Mexico City, have remained close friends and often spend long afternoons full of laughter with Jennifer Jones, my Vassar College classmate who I introduced to Pam when they both were living in Chicago. Soon after Pam and I ended our tours in Mexico City, we learned that our dear friend, Von, who had only a short time remaining before the end of her assignment, had tragically drowned in a freak accident in the swimming pool of the Princess Hotel in Acapulco.

My assignment after Mexico City was to be Dar es Salaam, Tanzania, and I returned to Washington, DC, to study the Kiswahili language and African Studies at the Foreign Service Institute. I had been accepted at, and deferred my admission to, graduate school at the Johns Hopkins School of Advanced International Studies (SAIS). As luck would have it, George Crowell, the same admissions person who had approached me in the hallway of B-CC High School to persuade me to attend Vassar College, was now the Assistant Dean at SAIS. He let me know before I returned from Mexico that if I did not enroll at SAIS as a full-time student in the fall, I would lose my partial fellowship. I recognized the importance of a graduate degree, particularly in a world and at a time when credentials and honors for achievement made an overrated impression on the power elite. I believe that, in most cases, my Vassar degree cum laude, Phi Beta Kappa induction, Master's Degree from SAIS, and work experience in the diplomatic corps always got me to the interview chair. Despite this, I inevitably saw that fleeting expression of confusion or surprise when the Lauri Fitz who walked through the door was not exactly the person the interviewer expected to see.

In short, I enrolled at SAIS and took the minimum number of courses required of full-time students. There was no part-time program in those days; the outcome was that the two-year program lasted four years, culminating with none other than Reverend Jesse Jackson as our commencement speaker in 1986. Along with graduate study, I began the grueling daily private Kiswahili classes for 3 to 4 hours each day. Although the language classes were intended to be followed by hours in the language lab, I skipped those to attend my classes at SAIS. I also attempted to reconnect with that tenuous, predominantly rocky long-distance relationship then in its ninth year with my boyfriend Ricky, from freshman year at Vassar who was now living in Washington, DC, and working at the Justice Department. Back in my hometown, I also tried to support the stressful health issues of other local members of my family.

My next assignment was to be US Press Attaché in Tanzania, the beloved country of President Julius Nyerere, Mwalimu (meaning "The Teacher" in Kiswahili). Tanzania was a country about which I had studied and the home of a president who I and many Africanists idolized. When apartheid was still enforced in South Africa, Tanzania was among the opposing "frontline states," the countries in southern Africa supporting an antiapartheid policy, one of disengagement with the apartheid government. At the time, the Reagan administration policy toward South Africa was "constructive engagement," a policy opposed to sanctions against South Africa and one that I interpreted as complicity. It conflicted with my strict antiapartheid moral and political code that I had developed over many years of protest. The United States Information Agency (USIA), at that time also known as USICA, was the branch of the Foreign Service where I was a diplomat. USIA's stated motto was, "telling America's story abroad." I was to be the press attaché or frequent public *face*, spokesperson, of the US Embassy in the capital of Dar es Salaam. I was one of the few Foreign Service Officers posted there who was required to learn Kiswahili, which would facilitate my interaction with the media and the public. The story America told abroad in 1982 was incomplete, revisionist, and neither a story I considered representative of the history nor the reality of Americans like me, people of color. If I were to be responsible for giving voice to my country's story, it needed to include my voice and those of many underrepresented in the narrative. Then, I was young, spirited, and lived in my truth. So, I exercised my kujichagulia (self-determination) and resigned from the Foreign Service.

My career counselor at USIA, Harriet Elam, a rising African American diplomat and role model, could not hide her disappointment when I walked into her office with my letter of resignation. She reminded me that I was privileged to be among the few who looked like us to serve our country as diplomats, of the responsibility I carried to uphold that honor for those who followed, and of the ancestors on whose shoulders I stood. I had not failed to consider those factors but had made up my mind; my path to critical decision-making is rarely without long contemplation and inner turmoil. I thanked her and walked out of her office completely sure of my decision. Harriet Elam-Thomas rose to be US Ambassador to Senegal, among her many other admirable career achievements. I was jobless, but I was living in my hometown and pursuing a graduate degree, so Ricky and

I moved in together to give our relationship a chance to lead to the marriage that we, and our families, expected.

Despite leaving the Foreign Service, I was gratified many years later when I met the venerated Ruth Davis, icon of the Foreign Service, the only African American woman to become Career Ambassador, the highest rank in the Foreign Service. I was honored to be invited to join Ambassador Davis as a senior advisor and mentor along with several other accomplished international affairs professionals of color. Over time three members of El Grupito (our group of junior officers in Santo Domingo), Lino, Pete, and Deborah, also became senior advisors at a program designed for mid-career international career professionals of color, the International Career Advancement Program (ICAP) established by University of Denver Professor Thomas Rowe over twenty years ago. Introduced to me by my friend and former assistant, who received her M.A. from the University of Denver, Charlotte Kea, this program has made a critical difference in the career paths and growth for hundreds of its participants. I have not only participated annually in the program but have continued to mentor dozens of its alumni. They have risen to impressive heights in their careers, including Foreign Service, nonprofit, policy institute, and private sector. They have often been invaluable to me in my work as have Tom, his wife Emita, and many of the other senior advisors who have grown to be close friends over the decades.

When Ambassador Davis heard my first presentation about my path from the career foreign service to a public relations executive, then return to government as a political appointee at Commerce, I was reminded of the day I resigned from the Foreign Service. She, like my USIA career counselor Harriet Elam, had a look on her face that questioned how I could have left a Foreign Service career. My career trajectory in and out of the government, and from career to political, was rare at that time. For some, it appeared not only unusual but also unfair to skirt the normal career path by gaining experience in the private sector and to reenter another branch of the Foreign Service as a senior official. However, again in the words of my mother's favorite Robert Frost poem, I took the "road less traveled."

CHAPTER FIVE

The 540

On April 10, 1996, President William Jefferson Clinton delivered a stirring eulogy at the National Cathedral for Ronald Harmon Brown, a man who had become his dear friend, became his Secretary of Commerce, and who, on a government plane with 35 others, had lost his life in service to the nation while on a trade mission to war-torn Croatia and Bosnia. President Clinton called Ron an "incredible life force" who "loved success," was "always so kind to people without regard to their station in life," and a man who had "lived a truly American life." He said Ron Brown was so "daring" that he, a man of African American heritage, would compete for the chairmanship of the Democratic National Committee, and against all the odds, win the position, becoming the first African American to head that organization . . . and then go on to get him elected president. To put no finer a point on his words, Bill Clinton said there were only two people who believed he could be president at the outset of his quest—his mother and Ron Brown.

Recalling Bill Clinton's powerful and deeply personal words helped crystallize my own thoughts about Ron

Brown. I met Ronald H. Brown in 1982 through an introduction by Florence Prioleau, a young lawyer at his firm Patton, Boggs, and Blow soon after I resigned from the Foreign Service and joined Gray and Company. She introduced me to Ron Brown, believing that my diplomatic background, service in the Dominican Republic, and new position at a cutting-edge public affairs firm might be just the combination of skill sets that he would find useful for a potential new client. Ron had been approached by the Haitian Government to work on several pressing issues in the bilateral relationship with the United States, and Ron, the consummate politician, likely also knew of the relationship of the chairman of my firm, Bob Gray, with President Reagan and his administration. Gray was cochair of the Reagan Inaugural and had been the cabinet secretary in President Eisenhower's administration. All these attributes made our first meeting both interesting and dynamic.

Even then, I could see that Ron was daring and an incredible life force; he brought the big ideas and was willing to think in a way that was limitless. Together we developed plans and strategies, moves and countermoves, and mapped out options. From that first meeting with Ron, my political life had begun, although I didn't know then that Ron Brown, a man who was living that extraordinary life, would be an ever-present force in mine from that moment on—and even after his untimely death.

Prior to joining Gray and Company and meeting Ron Brown, I had been a diplomat and therefore precluded from engagement in partisan politics. That changed when I began teaming up with Ron in 1982. He was steeped in Democratic politics, having been at the Urban League and on Capitol Hill working on the Judiciary Committee for Senator Ted Kennedy. I began working with him on many political events marking the beginning of my involvement in Democratic Party politics.

Ron emerged as a star from the Democratic Convention in 1988, where he was candidate for president, Jesse Jackson's convention manager, and I was Ron's press secretary. Nonetheless, his run for chairman of the Democratic Party was not easily achieved. There was opposition from several governors and countless strategy meetings to determine a path to victory. Several Democrats at Hill and Knowlton (H&K acquired Gray and Company around 1986) were involved in supporting Ron's candidacy. We and other advisors met in our conference room at H&K with colleagues, including campaign veteran and public relations expert Frank Mankiewicz. Meeting James Carville in one of those meetings left a lasting impression. The conference room with glass walls on every side but had an expansive a view of the Potomac River, and the Kennedy Center took on a different tenor with Carville taking up all the air in the room, dominating the conversation with his loud, thick Louisiana Cajun drawl laced with expletives. I always wondered what it would be like to be a fly on the wall of their home when those two well-known political personalities Carville, a Democratic operative and Mary Matlin, a GOP consultant, married.

Ron managed to win the support needed to become the first Black chairman of the Democratic Party in 1989. When Ron became chairman, I remained at Hill and Knowlton, but continued to volunteer my time and talents as he requested, supporting and accompanying him on trips to Europe and Africa and preparing his briefs for meetings with foreign leaders.

I accompanied Ron to the Liberal International in London in 1989. When working on his schedule, I always knew to include meetings with ruling and opposition parties wherever he visited. Our meeting with Gordon Brown, then emerging Labour Party leader who became Prime Minister in 2007, was particularly impressive, as was a meeting with a few Black members of Parliament.

Jim Hackney, an old friend of Ron's and mine, often laughed, and sometimes cried, about the situations we were forced to navigate for Ron and for ourselves on many occasions. A memorable one occurred in 1990. We were in Paris, en route home after a trip to several African nations that did not include a stop in Zaire because Mobutu Sese Seko, the infamous dictator and president of Zaire, was not in the country when we were expecting to meet with him. With little advance notice, however, we were invited to meet with President Mobutu at his residence in France. We traveled by small aircraft from Paris to Roquebrune-Cap-Martin, a commune secluded between Nice and Monaco.

Our car approached a long driveway leading to the estate that seemed paved in what appeared to be gold. We were shown the helicopter pad that somehow electronically rolled out a covering over the Olympic size swimming pool on the property where we were told we could land a helicopter on our next visit. Upon entering the home, we were blinded by crystal chandeliers. The massive dining table was set with the finest china, linen and lace napkins, and massive centerpieces of fragrant and exotic flowers. Welcoming us to his home, wearing his trademark leopard design kufi on his head, was His Excellency Mobutu Sese Seko. Leading a coup d'état in 1965, he remained the military dictator of what is now called the Democratic Republic of Congo, until 1997. His tenure was marked by human rights abuses, corruption, and alliances with the US, France, Belgium (the colonizers of the Congo), and China. The term "kleptocracy" was coined to describe his presidency. He was the host in Kinshasa of "Rumble in the Jungle," the epic boxing contest between Mohammed Ali and George Forman. To be sure, his extravagant French residence was no anomaly for his publicized lifestyle. Of course, Ron was never risk averse, and it was not out of character for him to meet with Mobutu; he believed in dialogue with everyone.

On our trip to Africa during Ron's tenure at the DNC, politics and commercial opportunities undergirded his discussions even then. He never visited a country without meeting with the opposition as well as the leadership in power. He made it a practice to venture into the marginalized communities, often becoming the first American leader these neighborhoods had ever glimpsed. He made it a point to engage with the youth and was often photographed surrounded by young children from Brazil to Senegal. Ron was well on his way to formulating what he would later incorporate as Secretary of Commerce into Clinton administration policy: using the path of "commercial diplomacy" to achieve diplomatic and economic gains.

Ron practiced the politics of equity and inclusion even before they became popular. He pursued and achieved ways to expand markets for US products. He displayed a dogged commitment to promoting international trade, facilitating relationships with emerging markets, leading trade missions to advocate aggressively for US business leaders—many of whom traveled with him—and to provide economic opportunities for small American businesses and underserved global communities. These trade missions generated criticism from some partisan quarters as vehicles to gain private sector support for the Democratic Party. Secretary Brown was always a magnet for controversy, but rarely did these allegations and attacks slow him down, although some of his highly competent and loyal staff grew weary of the consistent crisis management required by those working for him. His fortitude and compartmentalization were legendary among staff and soon were counted among his strongest characteristics.

My very first trip to the African continent had occurred in 1986, several years before the trip with DNC Chairman Brown, when my colleagues and I at Gray and Company traveled to Angola on a business trip. It seemed that the winds of change had begun to blow in Sub-Saharan Africa, and the continent was garnering increased American attention. Within the same year, I returned to Africa with Reverend Jesse Jackson and a relatively small delegation, including two of his children, Santita and Jesse, Jr.; some trusted business associates and friends; Ernie Green, one of the "Little Rock Nine;" a renowned musically gifted pastor, motivational speaker, and founder of the US Dream Academy, Wintley Phipps; Niger's Ambassador to the Organization of African Unity (OAU) Oumarou Youssoufou; and we who were staffing the trip, including Kgosie Matthews and Lezli Baskerville. In addition to the many historic meetings that took place, there were a number of amusing moments on that trip. Santita Jackson, Lezli, a rising attorney, and I were the only women on the trip. Lezli would later become the president and CEO of the National Association of Equal Opportunity in Higher Education. We somehow learned that someone had branded us "the Yum-Yum girls." It may have been an amusing sobriquet for some, but we considered it as clearly and entirely sexist.

A humorous moment came courtesy of one of the businessmen in the delegation who we nicknamed "Chief Uhuru" (uhuru means freedom in Kiswahili). When Botswana Foreign Minister Gaositwe Chiepe—who was among the first female foreign ministers in Africa, or perhaps in the world in 1986—met us at the Sun Hotel in Gaborone where the Botswana Government had chosen for us to spend the night, "Chief Uhuru" registered his loud and sustained dissatisfaction. The hotel chain was a target of criticism for their discriminatory practices in Africa, and Chief Uhuru refused to stay there. We were never sure where he slept that night but noticed the next morning at breakfast, a few cuts and bruises revealed signs of a rough night.

I returned to Botswana on several occasions later in

my career, for business meetings and conferences. The country became a destination of relative peace and stability in the Southern Africa Development Community (SADC). This trip was seminal for me beyond the incomparable meetings and period in history it marked. African nationalism among African American students was a strong current in many of our lives from our days on college campuses to how we conducted ourselves with friends and family. It influenced how we dressed (African garb was popular), how our hair blossomed into natural Afros framing our faces, and how we saluted each other with raised fists. We celebrated Kwanzaa; we spouted Swahili and Arabic phrases; we protested against apartheid in South Africa and for the freedom of Nelson Mandela; and we marched for the liberation of African countries and supported their struggle for independence from the yoke of colonialism. I was an avid student of African history, literature, and politics, so my commitment to learn about Africa and to follow developments on the continent has been a lifelong practice. The Constituency for Africa (CFA), founded and headed by Mel Foote, for decades has advocated for Africa and those in the Diaspora. I have supported CFA's agenda and appreciate its consistent and long-standing recognition of the importance of the African Diaspora in the US and worldwide. I continue my involvement with the African Policy Group (APG) founded by Vivian Lowery Derrick, a respected former assistant administrator for Africa of the US Agency for International Development. The bipartisan APG is replete with African scholars, former US Ambassadors to countries in Africa, and high-level officials from several US government agencies, and private sector and nonprofit leaders, who are all consumed with advocating for countries and issues essential for a healthy political and economic future for the continent.

It was a pleasure to travel with Reverend Jackson in 1986,

Reverend Jesse Jackson
and Lauri

an American leader with whom I could share my commitment to the African continent. The trip was two years after his first run for president and two years before his second run, which proved even more historic. In 1988, Jackson beat Senators Gore and Biden and Congressman Gephardt, and came in second only to Governor Dukakis in number of delegates as he approached the Democratic National Convention in Atlanta. (This was twenty years before Barack Obama was elected. Few will forget the look on Reverend Jackson's face when the television camera panned to him at the historic inauguration of President Barack Obama.)

Jackson was the master of quotable and memorable oratory. In his 1988 Convention speech, comparing himself to nominee Dukakis, he said:

> *Providence has enabled our paths to intersect. His fore parents came to America on immigrant ships: my fore parents came to America on slave ships. But whatever the original ships, we're in the same boat tonight.*

He ended that speech with what became his mantra, "Keep hope alive." Despite it being ridiculed by some as trite, it was quite meaningful at that moment in history:

> *Wherever you are tonight, you can make it. Hold your head high, stick your chest out. You can make it. It gets dark sometimes, but the morning comes. Don't you surrender! Suffering breeds character, character breeds*

faith. In the end faith will not disappoint. You must not surrender! You may or may not get there but just know that you're qualified! And you hold on and hold out!

We must never surrender!! America will get better and better. Keep hope alive! Keep hope alive!

Keep hope alive!

On the trip to multiple countries of Africa in 1986, Jesse Jackson did his homework. He spoke substantively about the issues and presented worthy proposals for cooperation and potential change. He had an inimitable rocking movement from foot to foot, side to side, when he delivered a speech or sermon. His voice slowly reached a crescendo; his movements matched the reverberating rhythm of his words. The audiences were captured, hypnotized in the moment. It was his 540, in ballet, a spectacular leap, soaring high from the stage, with an astounding twist in the air, that was usually performed by male dancers with confidence and bravado.

An example of his consistent resistance to the apartheid regime in South Africa, Reverend Jackson said in that same 1988 Democratic Convention speech:

We have basic challenges—freedom in South Africa. We've already agreed as Democrats to declare South Africa to be a terrorist state. But don't just stop there. Get South Africa 1986 out of Angola: free Namibia: support the front-line states. We must have a new humane human rights consistent policy in Africa.

On the 1986 trip with "Reverend" (which he was called with respect by those who knew him well) en route to the continent, we had a layover in London and took the opportunity to set the tone for our upcoming journey by joining an antiapartheid protest. Our group protests continued after we arrived in Africa as well. Upon getting to Botswana, we received an unexpected invitation to Bishop Desmond Tutu's investiture in South Africa. During apartheid in South Africa, the designation of "Honorary White" was afforded selectively to people of color in order to receive the rights and privileges to which they otherwise would not receive. Our African American delegation would have been designated as such for entry to South Africa. We graciously declined. Instead, we continued our antiapartheid protest by congregating at the heavily guarded South Africa-Botswana border. With only security forces as our puzzled but peaceful observers, Reverend led us in prayer for Bishop Tutu, and for freedom for Mandela and the people of South Africa.

Emblazoned in my mind are Reverend's fiery and inspirational speeches in the capitals of the African countries we visited. We had intimate and memorable meetings with legendary leaders and presidents: Nigeria's Ibrahim Babangida, Kenneth Kaunda of Zambia, Zimbabwe's Robert Mugabe, and Botswana's Quett Masire. President Kaunda welcomed us to his residence with its expansive grounds full of beautiful plants and wildlife. Kaunda was a conservationist who was unsuccessful in stemming poaching during his tenure. As he welcomed us, I smiled as I noticed his trademark white handkerchief in his left hand, which he used to wipe his tears when making speeches about the challenges of Africa.

We also met with Samora Machel, president of Mozambique, who died in a plane crash soon thereafter. His widow, Graça Machel, later married Nelson Mandela. She exudes purpose, wisdom, and elegance. I have long admired her.

We learned that our own plane was almost shot down upon crossing the border into Angolan airspace due to a glitch in preclearance. In war-torn Angola, we met MPLA leader José Eduardo dos Santos, whom I had met a few months prior during my business trip to Luanda with my Gray and Company colleagues. At Futongo, dos Santos' compound, we met exiled Namibia freedom fighters Sam Nujoma and Ben Gurirab, dressed in full camouflage fatigues. I was in awe of meeting actual revolutionaries about whom I had only read.

Each day on that trip created another cherished memory. As we drove from Dar es Salaam to Dodoma, I was overjoyed at the prospect of meeting the leader I had studied as a college student. We were greeted by "Mwalimu," the name of respect and reverence given to Julius Nyerere. The aging former Tanzanian president was moving slowly, but his mind was sharp, and our group sat talking in his living room at his home in Dodoma. He and his "Ujamaa Villages" (local people cooperating with each other to provide essentials for living and sharing profits, cooperative economics) made famous during his presidency had been a focus in my African Studies curriculum at Vassar and contributed to my later decision to leave the Foreign Service. I never dreamed that I would meet and speak with him in the intimacy of his home only a decade later.

Neither could I have imagined that just a few years later, in 1990, when I again traveled to Africa with Chairman Ron Brown, that we would sit at the dinner table of President Sam Nujoma with Foreign Minister Ben Gurirab (married to the accomplished Joan Weston Guriras, an African American). We were the first Americans to dine with the newly independent Namibia's leaders. I had participated in many antiapartheid and African Liberation Day marches in the years prior to those trips to Africa. Meeting so many presidents of newly liberated and independent African nations was thrilling and such a privilege during those historic and hopeful years.

My most impactful and treasured meeting, however, was on that 1990 trip with Ron to South Africa. We had the privilege of meeting with Nelson Mandela. We were among the first American delegations to meet with "Madiba" just months after he was released from Robben

From left: Lauri, Ron Brown, and Nelson Mandela

Island. It was a very significant trip for us all, but particularly special was meeting him in his humble home in Soweto, with Winnie Mandela emerging briefly from the kitchen to greet Ron and his wife Alma, along with Lynn Cutler (who was a vice chair of the DNC), Bill Morton, Ron's ever-faithful right hand (who later died with him), and me. The song "Bring Him Back Home" by the famous South African musician, Hugh Masekela, which had become an anthem for many of us united with South Africans in the struggle, the Free South Africa Movement, resounded in my head as I reached over to shake Mandela's hand; "Bring back Nelson Mandela/ Bring him back to Soweto/ I wan't to see him walking down the streets of South Africa (Tomorrow)." And here I was with this venerable icon in his home in Soweto.

I am reminded of the fact that Arthur Ashe, my dad's close friend who had stayed at our home as a young tennis player participating in the annual DC Tennis Tournament, was the victim of criticism when he accepted a visa designating him "Honorary White" status. That designation was required so he could travel to South Africa to make a statement against apartheid from inside its borders. Ashe was an early model of an athlete who dared to use his celebrity to draw attention to roiling political issues. After nervously serving him the dinner

Mom had prepared, with his favorite orange soda, he invited me to ride with him to attend his tennis match. On that day, my mom was not at home, and tennis player Stan Smith, who was also staying with us, had left after losing his match. My dad had headed out early to be a linesman or umpire at the tournament, which he had done for years at many tournaments, including being a linesman at Wimbledon. That day, I was wide-eyed when I spotted Diana Ross in a bright yellow pants suit, much thinner than she appeared on television, who had come to see Arthur Ashe play. A few years later, my dad and I attended his wedding, when he married the talented and beautiful photographer Jeannie Moutoussamy. Their wedding was officiated by Dad's Howard University classmate, Andrew Young. Years later, but much too soon, we all mourned Arthur Ashe's death at the young age of fifty-four after he became infected with HIV after a tainted blood transfusion.

Those were the years when the AIDS epidemic began to ravish so many communities in the US. Early in the search for its origin and cure, it was referred to as "4-H" disease—attributed to Haitians, Hemophiliacs, Heroin users, and Homosexuals. One of Gray and Company's tasks on behalf of the Haitian Government was to secure the removal of the reference to Haitians from the stigmatizing and derogatory 4-H designation.

Our work for Haiti was coordinated under the guidance of the Haitian Ambassadors to the US, George Leger and later Fritz Cineas, and the Foreign Minister Jean-Robert Estimé who remains a friend. Ron and I pursued many objectives for the country, including increased aid, inclusion of Haiti receiving benefits of the Caribbean Basin Initiative, an important trade agreement with the region, and fighting for removal of the Haitian people from the 4-H designation. Haiti faced discrimination in the US where Haitian immigrants were pejoratively labeled "boat people" and, unlike arriving Cuban immigrants, were not welcomed and afforded refugee status with an immediate path to green cards and US citizenship.

We organized and led delegations of Americans to Haiti from the private sector and arts community. I had the honor of attending to the famous African American dancer Geoffrey Holder (who was married to the still breathtakingly beautiful former dancer Carmen de Lavallade) when he visited Haiti. Another dancer, Katherine Dunham, called the "matriarch and queen mother of Black dance, was best known for her relationship to Haiti. She was a dancer, choreographer, anthropologist, educator, and social activist. Dunham traveled extensively throughout the world, and during her travels and study of dance in the Caribbean, she was drawn to return to Haiti many times to study Vodun (an African derived religious tradition) rituals, with a focus on the dance. I had an occasion to visit what was her oasis for living and creating in Port-au-Prince. It was easy to understand the creativity and inexplicable magic she must have discovered in Haiti. The cultural richness of the country is lost to many who have not explored it and focus only on the tragic political, economic, and natural disasters that plague the country. I likely would have been more nervous had Mr. Holder's wife, Carmen de Lavallade, accompanied him on that trip. When I saw her a few years ago at Arthur Mitchell's homegoing, I could only stare in utter awe when she floated to the podium to deliver remarks in all her majestic elegance at age eighty-seven.

I was particularly informed and sensitized to the HIV/AIDS crisis early on because Gray and Company was early on an avant-garde public affairs company. Housed in the Powerhouse Building in the toney DC neighborhood of Georgetown, and founded by Robert K. Gray, many of my male colleagues were gay and activists, not so com-

monplace in the early '80s. Bob Gray was a major supporter of Robert Gallo, a critical researcher and contrib-
utor to discoveries related to HIV and AIDS as well as of
Anthony Fauci who has spent decades focused on treatments for the disease long before being recognized for
his work on COVID-19.

Among my former Gray and Company colleagues and
friends who have continued their activism are:

- Bob Witeck has been active in LGBTQ civil rights for
  four decades. After leaving Gray and Company, thirty
  years ago he launched the nation's first certified gay-
  owned business in the US and wrote the first book on
  gay communications. He has advised leading Fortune
  100 corporations including American Airlines, Marri-
  ott, Walmart, and Ford, on their LGBTQ business and
  marketing strategies.

- Jeff Trammell launched his own public policy shop in
  Washington, DC, and dedicated much of his time to
  pro bono LGBTQ advocacy working with Democratic
  presidential and Senate campaigns. He made history
  as the first openly gay Rector of his alma mater, the
  College of William & Mary; he and his longtime partner, Stuart Serkin, were married by former justice
  and then William & Mary chancellor, the Honorable
  Sandra Day O'Connor.

- And Charles Francis, following his long career as a corporate communications strategist, revived the gay activist nonprofit, the DC Mattachine Society. The Mattachine Society was originally founded by gay pioneer, Dr.
  Frank Kameny in the 1950s. However, after Francis and
  Bob Witeck preserved decades of Kameny's papers in
  the Library of Congress and Smithsonian, Francis used
  this platform for "archival activism" to retrieve, resur-
  rect, and use all forms of hidden LGBTQ documents,
  artifacts, and records to advance civil rights litigation,
  legislation, and movements.

Secretary of Commerce
Ronald H. Brown

We all lost colleagues and/or their partners in these
early stages of that deadly disease. I shared the grief suffered by those who lost loved ones, the fight to secure
funding for HIV research, and the miracle of survival for
those who benefitted from developing treatments. I had
developed an enduring bond with many of those Gray
and Company and Hill and Knowlton colleagues during
the '80s and early '90s prior to joining the Clinton administration.

In 1993, Ronald Harmon Brown was confirmed as
Secretary of Commerce in the Clinton administration,
although he truly had wanted to be Secretary of State.
He was initially offered the position of Ambassador to
the United Nations, which would have required him to
move to New York. The position would not have been the
first for an African American, as both Andrew Young and
Donald McHenry served as US Ambassadors to the United Nations previously. Ron relished being the first. Nonetheless, during inner circle discussions I supported him
accepting that position as a possible path to Secretary of
State, a position he hoped to have one day. It also would
take him back to his native New York where he could
renew his contacts and build a constituency for any fu-

ture political aspirations, although moving to New York might have presented a hardship for his family. While he entertained the possibility, in his research about the reporting lines for UN Ambassador, he learned that there was precedent for that position to report directly to the president rather than to the new Secretary of State. Warren Christopher, objected to what he must have felt was potential circumvention of his authority, so Ron instead opted to accept the role of Secretary of Commerce. Ron explained why he had ended his pursuit of the UN Ambassadorship and told me that he was on his way to the airport for a hasty announcement in Little Rock. It seems that President Clinton had decided to bundle the announcement of the Secretary of Commerce with several other cabinet appointments. Ron always had the ability to turn on a dime and not look back. Later, I recall that some of the people who had been with him when he accepted the nomination said that he had asked them, "What exactly does the Secretary of Commerce do?" Ron would constantly give us reason to chuckle and sometimes even to laugh out loud.

Ron was committed to providing opportunities for young people, women, and people of color. His circle at Commerce became the gold standard for exceptional and diverse talent. He hired people who have gone on to do extremely meaningful things in subsequent years, and some who would have, had they not died very young in service to him and the country on that fateful plane crash in 1996. He debunked the too-often repeated comment of many white people, "Well, I can't find any minorities to hire with the capabilities, background, or experience"—to Ron Brown, that was utter nonsense.

One day at Commerce in 1994, after I had become Assistant Secretary and Director General of the US and Foreign Commercial Service, Secretary Brown's ever loyal and competent assistant Barbara Schmitz who had worked with him since his Patton, Boggs and Blow days, called me in my office to tell me that the Secretary needed to meet with me. Never knowing what new task Ron might ask of me, I entered his inner sanctum. That day he asked me to meet with a young African American woman named Susan Rice who was relatively new to her position at the National Security Council as Special Assistant for Africa. He explained that she had grown up in his neighborhood, that he knew and respected her parents, and that she was very talented and might appreciate meeting with me, another African American woman with a decade more experience in the spaces of government, politics, and the private sector. Susan and I hit it off immediately from our quiet lunch in the White House mess. Susan would soon become a first-time mother and navigate that difficult space between personal drive and being expected to excel in all aspects of life's unique challenges—a particularly lonely road for women like us.

From that day, we have shared many personal and professional experiences: from Secretary Brown's inclusive interagency trips to Africa when she was at the State Department as Assistant Secretary of State for African Affairs in 1995, to the poignant ceremony in 2011, fifteen years after his death, when US Ambassador to the United Nations, Susan Rice, presided over the room packed with teary eyed former employees, friends, and family of the late Secretary Brown to name the US. Mission to the United Nations in Ron's honor. Susan and I campaigned together for Obama; I attended her legendary annual Christmas parties; our children attended the same school; together we watched in awe when the Queen of Soul Aretha Franklin was the surprise guest at her fiftieth birthday party; and I sent supportive missives to her when she was under fire, as well as notes of congratulations as she has continued to serve our country. But the best times of all are when we share what we both enjoy,

From left: Pedro Alfonso, Ron Brown, Wandra Mitchell, and Lauri

time to let it "all hang out" and just dance.

Ron had a way of finding and connecting people at the right time and for the right reasons. He always extended his embrace and support well beyond "The Talented Tenth," a twentieth-century term for a leadership class of Black people. It was an incomparable moment in time and in history. He landed more 540s—spectacular leaps—in his lifetime than anyone can count. Spectators do not always fully recognize or appreciate how difficult it is to perform that move.

During the last six months of his life, Ron practically circled the globe leading trade missions and advocating for US companies. He had afforded a great deal of time and energy to his special commitment to Africa by leading the first US trade mission to South Africa upon the lifting of US sanctions and later opening the first US Commercial Service (FCS) office in Johannesburg. Each Secretary of Commerce was able to name only one appointment of a senior official in a country of his choice. He chose South Africa and appointed my long-time friend Millard Arnold, former executive director of the Southern Africa Project at the Lawyers Committee for Civil Rights, Deputy Assistant Secretary of State for Human Rights and Humanitarian Affairs, and Professor of Law and Senior Fellow at the Carnegie Endowment for International Peace.

And as Ron had done in all the other major global emerging markets, we established new commercial office hubs in several major African capitals. Ron also facilitated trade and commercial opportunities for the US and South Africa by convening around the same table for the first time in Washington, DC, white and Black South Africans with US businesses to form the US-South Africa Business Council. Many of us who staffed and observed the proceedings from a bird's-eye view basked in the glow of the dynamic fraternal energy between Secretary Brown and his South African counterpart Trevor Manuel, Minister of the Department of Trade and Industry. Their bond was immediate and lasting, a true friendship of "brothers from another mother." Trevor genuinely mourned Ron's death and those he came to know on his staff who also perished in that crash. The mention of Ron Brown's name to the many Africans and Americans who participated in and benefitted from his efforts generates nostalgic smiles and gratitude. When he died, he was recognized and grieved by a great many African leaders.

On Ron's last trip to the African continent, we traveled to Ghana, Senegal, Kenya, and South Africa, meeting delegations of businesspeople at each stop to advocate for US companies and facilitating commercial relationships. During that period, we also went to the Middle East. I recounted a few years ago at a dinner in Jordan with fellow Trustees from Global Communities, an international nonprofit organization working to improve the lives of vulnerable communities worldwide, that when I was with Ron in his last months, we had three meetings in less than 72 hours with Yitzhak Rabin, Yasser Arafat, and King Hussein. Those were hopeful times for resolution of the seemingly endless Middle East crisis, as Ron totally embodied his distinct role as interlocutor and envoy for President Clinton. Within weeks of that meeting, Rabin would be killed; not five months later, Ron would be dead. Those were "heady" years witnessing Ron Brown's inimitable magic, and his light was extinguished way too soon.

Ron's final trip was leading a delegation of American company representatives to discuss rebuilding destroyed infrastructure in Bosnia and Croatia. He flew to Tuzla, Bosnia, to meet with US troops stationed there and took them McDonald's hamburgers. From there he was to fly to Dubrovnik to discuss rebuilding Croatia's tourism infrastructure. It was on that leg of the journey that forces conspired, including weather, equipment failure, pilot error, and destiny, to crash his plane into St. John's Mountain a few days before Easter on April 3, 1996.

My Senior Commercial Officer based in Taiwan intercepted me as I transited on my hurried trip back to DC from Vietnam where I had been when the news hit CNN and we received calls from hysterical friends and colleagues in Washington. Pilar Martinez, my rock and assistant who came with me to Commerce from Hill and Knowlton (and who was with me in three of my positions over twenty years), kept me informed of what was happening in Washington, while she managed dozens of phone calls to my office from friends and family. At my home, my frightened and overwhelmed teenage son was responding to a flurry of calls as well. Pilar handled every crisis with calm and quiet strength. She is loyal and trustworthy, and always there. Without her support and friendship, I might have drowned amid the many challenges in my professional and personal life.

When the crash occurred, we were in the midst of opening the first US Commercial Service Office since the Vietnam War, and my colleague Undersecretary Tim Hauser and I were leading a US business delegation. As we received the news about the crash, we huddled in a hotel suite to learn as much as became available, it was strangely comforting to see the equally pained expressions of my colleagues and friends. They included Katie Moore, who I had hired at Hill and Knowlton, and had joined me at Commerce, and Jim Desler, a fellow Ron Brown's disciple, also staffing the trip to Vietnam. At that point, it was still a search and rescue mission, with a possibility that the plane had crashed into the Adriatic and that some passengers had survived.

I was paged as I landed in Taiwan and was handed a phone to speak to Mary Fran Kirchner, a colleague on my staff in Washington. I was hoping the call was about survivors of the crash. Instead, she asked if I would detour to Dubrovnik to represent the Department of Commerce and the Brown family. I knew I was being asked to fill this special role for several reasons. Alexis Herman, Clinton White House Director of the Office of Public Liaison (later Secretary of Labor) and friend who was close to Ron and his family, was managing the events from Washington and knew that Ron's wife Alma, and his family, trusted me. They also knew what I had come to learn, especially on this painful journey—that I was respected by my colleagues at Commerce and elsewhere in the administration, and that I could use my hard-earned experience in complex international situations to navigate even this most difficult one. I of course agreed to fly to Zagreb, not knowing what duties would be required of me, or whether the crash was fatal for all; amid the possible added emotional dimension of losing my friend and mentor, several of my own staff, other colleagues and friends with whom I had worked in the trenches for years, and the corporate executives who were on a business mission to do good for a devastated region. I prepared myself by releasing my pent-up emotions and anxiety in welcomed anonymity among

Crash site, Dubrovnik, Croatia, *AP PHOTO / Enric Marti*

airline passengers as my tears flowed during the seemingly interminable flights from Taiwan to Dubrovnik.

Upon my arrival in Zagreb, I entered a dark and bottomless sea of grief, whose creatures comprised a group of young Commerce Department "advance" staff. Knowing that no words could touch the depths of our pain, I asked that we all join hands in prayer to whatever higher power in whom we believed, both for the victims and for us as survivors, recognizing perhaps subconsciously that we would long be plagued by "survivor guilt" and PTSD, as those who, but for the vicissitudes of fate, might have been on that plane.

I finally landed in Dubrovnik from Zagreb in a Croatian government aircraft. With me was a particularly shaken Morris Reid, who shared his story of only escaping that fatal crash because of a reprimand from Ron prior to his departure from Zagreb on the leg to Tuzla. Ron delivered Morris strict instructions to remain in Zagreb to resolve an unfinished task and to later fly to Dubrovnik to meet the incoming delegation's flight from Tuzla.

In Dubrovnik, we were met by and encountered the most kind, gracious, and empathetic local officials and community. They were overwrought that these Americans, coming to help rebuild their country, had perished in their city. Some reflected on the fact that, a few weeks earlier, two American officials had died in a car crash a few miles outside of Dubrovnik.

US military troops flew in from Italy for the recovery. They took me up to the crash site by helicopter where the only sight I chose to recall was the completely intact tail of the Air Force plane miraculously and still pristinely emblazoned with the American flag. The view from that point on the mountainside was a devastatingly spectacular picture of the iconic ancient city of Dubrovnik bordering a calm, hauntingly beautiful, Adriatic Sea.

I asked the pilot if he would take a picture of the view from the crash site of the town and the Adriatic Sea and send it to me. He did, and I duplicated the photo and sent it to the victims' families with a note of sympathy, explaining that I was a US government designated official from Commerce, who, along with a few other government staff and the Croatian Ambassador to the United States, had accompanied their loved one home.

We flew with 33 US flag-draped coffins in the hull of a freezing cold C-130 transport plane from Dubrovnik to Dover Delaware Air Force Base; two others who perished were Croatian and were buried in Dubrovnik. At the Dover landing, we were met by President and Hillary Clinton, Vice President and Tipper Gore, White House staff, Commerce staff, and the families—mothers, fathers, children, spouses, brothers, sisters, colleagues, and friends of those whose American flag-draped coffins were ceremonially unloaded, one by one. It was a gathering of unfathomable despair. Morris Reid and I were escorted to a holding room where Ron's family—wife Alma, son Michael, and daughter Tracy, with their spouses—awaited us. Morris gave them Ron's unscathed and working watch and his hardly damaged famous leather binder, which held his briefing book. The irony of these items surviving the devastating crash was cause for a shared smile in that moment of tremendous grief.

I somehow hoped that the families, when they eventually worked through their various stages of grief, could find some small degree of solace in the photograph of the juxtaposed beauty of the mountain peak captured in that shot of the crash. Years later, I hiked up that rocky and difficult to ascend hillside to the majestic monument, erected in honor of the victims. I imagined how hard it must have been for the recovery teams to get there and to descend with the victims' remains, attempting it in the rain and with the possibility of tripping a stray land-mine. I heard that there was one survivor, a flight atten-dant, who had been found trapped under an airline cart, and who later perished on the descent down that hill.

The global staff I led at the Department of Commerce was largely responsible for the Secretary's advance and on-the-ground logistical support when he traveled. I had therefore traveled with him on many of these trips, includ-ing to a dozen countries within the last six months of his life. On that difficult return to Dover with the remains, I realized this would be my last trip forever with Ron. I sat with the Croatian Ambassador to the US, Miomir Zuzul, on a hard straight-backed jump seat across from a few silent Commerce colleagues for 13 hours. Initially, as I boarded the plane after the departure ceremony with the troops, President Tudjman, and US Ambassador Peter Galbraith, I was escorted to a seat reserved for me in the cockpit. When we took off and ascended into the clouds, the view was a limitless expanse of white space. I couldn't bear to continue in that confined space, alone and lost in my own thoughts. I left my seat and stepped down into the sea of American flags, when I focused for the first time on Commerce De-partment colleagues Morris Reid, Ira Sokowitz, and one of my senior FCS officers Bob Taft, seated on one side of the coffins, and on the other side of the plane was a distraught man I soon learned was the recently appointed Croatian Ambassador to Washington, Miomir Zuzul. I introduced myself and took the seat beside him. While the flight was interminable, we talked for hours, consciously focusing our gaze on each other to avoid the morbid sight before us. That conversation bonded us for years to come. My life and the lives of so many others were changed during that long flight home.

Survivor's guilt is traumatic, and it was ever present as I attended and spoke at so many funerals for my friends and colleagues. Andrew Balfour, on my staff, so ably articulated my thoughts and crafted many of my remarks into appropriate prose. Today, I try to avoid attending funerals, not out of a lack of respect for the departed one and family, but because of the collateral damage that remains in my heart. Charlotte Kea, my special assistant, was a constant source of comfort with her gentle and sensitive demeanor, despite her own grief, as she, also, lost many friends and colleagues. Charlotte often traveled as advance staff for these trips, and before joining me had worked closely with the Secretary as assistant to the Counselor Jim Hackney. I was so thankful for her support, as Ron's death, and the deaths of so many with him, had left me mentally and physically exhausted. I felt compelled to soldier on and didn't realize that I, too, needed the time to process the pain and to recover; the grieving process is critical and can't be shortened or ignored. The understanding and clarity about its impact on our minds and hearts escaped me then.

Ron died the way he had lived: taking risks with compartmentalized abandon, with his signature optimism and belief that he could control any outcome. Unfortunately, this time, it was not to be.

CHAPTER SIX

Contretemps

Sometime in 1619, a Portuguese slave ship, the São João Bautista, traveled across the Atlantic Ocean with a hull filled with human cargo: captive Africans from Angola, in southwestern Africa. The men, women and children, most likely from the kingdoms of Ndongo and Kongo, endured the horrific journey, bound for a life of enslavement in Mexico. Almost half the captives had died by the time the ship was seized by two English pirate ships; the remaining Africans were taken to Point Comfort, a port near Jamestown, the capital of the English colony of Virginia, which the Virginia Company of London had established 12 years earlier. The colonist John Rolfe wrote to Sir Edwin Sandys, of the Virginia Company, that in August 1619, a "Dutch man of war" arrived in the colony and "brought not anything but 20 and odd Negroes, which the governor and cape merchant bought for victuals." The Africans were most likely put to work in the tobacco fields that had recently been established in the area.

—New York Times Magazine,
"The 1619 Project," August 19, 2019

When I resigned from the Foreign Service in 1982, with no idea what I would do, I was hired that same year by the public affairs company, Gray and Company. A few years later, in 1986, Gray and Company was hired by the Marxist Party for the Liberation of Angola (MPLA) to establish the groundwork for normalization of the trade relationship with the United States. I went to Angola for the first time on a business trip with three Gray and Company colleagues; Dr. Gerald Bender, a professor at UCLA and recognized scholar on Angola also joined us in Luanda. While in the country, we were escorted by an entourage of exceedingly personable Angolans on a fascinating journey through several provinces of war-torn, but still beautiful, Angola. We met with and had discussions with local officials and residents, and inhaled the breathtaking landscape of ocean, hillsides, and desert of Angola, a country stained by civil war.

On one stop at a huge rally on a stage with MPLA officials, when the massive crowd began a customary and rousing "call and response," my colleague, Ronna Freiberg, and I stood nervously with two senior Gray and Company colleagues. One was the conservative former commander of the 6th Fleet, Chief of Staff to George H.W. Bush and Deputy Director of the CIA, Admiral Daniel J. Murphy; the other was Frank Mankiewicz, renowned Democratic operative, Bobby Kennedy's press secretary, and public relations advisor extraordinaire. They both, with raised fist, joined the Angolan officials and the crowd in chanting the famous liberation phrase I had learned in college and that we frequently chanted as a battle cry of unity at the conclusion of our frequent campus protests, "A Luta Continua" in Portuguese, meaning "the struggle continues." Frank, who spoke Spanish, likely was familiar with the popular freedom fighters' chant, but I'm sure Admiral Murphy did not grasp the significance of the words as he enthusiastically shouted them, or the significance of his fist raised in solidarity with our Marxist clients. Frank was an indescribable force of nature who was widely admired and who shared his wisdom and humor with so many of us until his death. Admiral Murphy, head of Gray and Company's International Division and my boss at the time, had a highly accomplished professional record and had served his nation in many positions. As both are now deceased, it is likely we will never know what each was thinking at the time. The image of the two of them on that stage is seared into my brain.

Social media did not exist at the time, so little in the way of photographic evidence exists, and even less is known about how Charlie Black, Paul Manafort, Roger Stone, and Peter Kelly (of the lobbying firm, Black Manafort, Stone and Kelly, or BMSK) applied quite shrewd tactics in their representation of Jonas Savimbi of the opposing UNITA party, who was then supported by the Reagan administration and viewed as a freedom fighter. Soon after, my colleagues and I returned from our trip to Angola where we had been showered with the unexpectedly warm Angolan hospitality and had met with MPLA leadership from Party Leader José Eduardo dos Santos to provincial and town leaders and had committed to a program in conjunction with our contact, MPLA Trade Minister Ismael Martins. Upon our return to the US, an incredibly vocal group of protesters expressed their outrage about Gray and Company's work for the MPLA. I always believed this student protest and subsequent negative press was instigated by BMSK to pressure my Republican colleagues into abandoning our commitment to the MPLA. To my great embarrassment, they were successful, and Gray and Company senior leadership decided to abandon the client. The war in Angola was not front-page news and the press had not spent much ink on it. So, to see American protesters (primarily students) carrying signs accusing our firm of being "Commies and Marxists" outside of our offices at The Powerhouse and the Flour Mill on a quiet street in Georgetown, with some even dramatically chaining themselves to the railings outside of our buildings, was shocking.

We managed to secure a second opportunity to represent Angola a few years later when Gray and Company had been acquired by Hill and Knowlton. I was by then head of the international division, and it fell largely on the shoulders of my colleague, Jill Schuker, and me to develop the strategy and to implement the path toward Angola's goal of full US diplomatic recognition. We painstakingly and carefully crafted a deliberate plan contributing to the establishment of Angola's first Embassy in Washington, DC. Our efforts were instrumental in gaining approval for the first Angolan Ambassador in Washington, José Patricio, for whom we provided much-needed and continuous advice and support in that critical phase of a new and unprecedented bilateral relationship. We also supported the first visit of President dos Santos of Angola to the United States, and continuously advocated for the US government's official and full recognition of Angola. Jill and I worked seamlessly with the daily responsibility of shifting strategies, designing innovative approaches, explaining US policy developments, monitoring constant and complicated developments in the capital, Luanda, and crafting messages, responses, and press releases. This effort required the advice and support of other colleagues at Hill and Knowlton, including my diligent staff and colleagues Diana Aldridge and later Toby Moffett. Finally, in 1993, before I joined the Clinton administration, we proudly celebrated the establishment of full diplomatic relations between the United States and Angola, allowing each country to enjoy all of the ceremonial and the substantial political, economic, and strategic benefits of this groundbreaking relationship.

It was on my first trip to Luanda in 1986 that I met my future husband, an Angolan and divorced father of two children. He was eight years my senior and had a heart of gold. This marked a life-changing contretemps. In ballet, contretemps is a quick movement of the feet executed with a small jump and shift of weight that changes the direction of the subsequent movement. Fernando Pegado certainly brought with him a definitive change of direction for my heart and in my life.

I had spent many years of my life in Africa-focused study, protesting apartheid, supporting sanctions against South Africa, and advocating for the liberation of African countries from colonialism and exploitation. I also strongly identified with the African Diaspora with all its symbolic and policy implications. So, here I was, as all of this culminated in a moment of truth. With Fernando, I found a home for my passions. I not only gained a partner, but a direct family linkage to Angola, the land of the first-documented record of Africans to blaze the blood and tear-stained road into enslavement; it had been America's contretemps.

Fernando and I were married on Memorial Day Weekend in 1988. I was attracted to his worldliness, his kindness, and his impeccable taste from interior decorating to fashion. We had compatible political views and en-

Lauri and Fernando,
London, 1988

gaged in stimulating conversations together and with family and friends. It was a whirlwind romance with a good man who was attentive, loving, and generous in every way to everyone. He was a fantastic cook, and my mother often mused that he should open a restaurant.

I was an independent thirty-three-year-old, with twelve years international career experience. I believed myself to be well traveled, but even I was in awe after meeting Fernando and learning that this man had been to the far corners of the globe and had seen and savored fruits and had experiences I only imagined existed. He had a deep appreciation and interest in things important to me: world affairs, the politics of inclusion, arts and culture, travel, and design. The clothes he enjoyed buying me on his travels were always fashionable, exceptionally beautiful, and a perfect fit. He was the right man, at the right time for a new and exciting adventure, as I entered a new chapter in my life.

My father had told me repeatedly over the years, perhaps in jest—but knowing him, he was probably serious—that when I decided to marry, I should elope. The ever-obedient daughter, I did elope and was married in London at Marylebone Town Hall where my only guests and witnesses were Mark Shepherd, a dear English client in the banknote business who had become a friend, and his wife, Alice. Mark has remained a good friend over the years as we have shared mutual friendships through introductions we facilitated for each other, shared stories of adventures and interests in countries throughout the globe, and our affinity for Africa. It was Mark who introduced me almost twenty years ago to now Ghanaian President Nana Akufo-Ado. Over the years I have heard the president speak during visits to the US and have been hosted by him and his wife at their home in Accra. Rosa Whitaker accomplished African American businesswoman, Africa advocate, former colleague, and friend, and her husband Ghanaian Archbishop Nicholas Duncan Williams have invited me to events in Washington, DC, that they have hosted for President Akufo-Ado.

After the short official marriage ceremony, our guests attended a lovely luncheon I had arranged just the day before for my husband's friends, his young daughter, and his youngest sister. I had met these family members already and knew many of the guests. I was flabbergasted at how a wedding could be arranged in 48 hours and appear to have been planned for months. Because it took place over the Memorial Day holiday, I had three lovely days away from work; the weekend had been flawless and exciting. My only major disappointment was that my British wedding certificate classified me as a *spinster*!

My family adjusted to the relatively short courtship and marriage. They had taken for granted that Ricky and I—after our ten-year relationship through college, my time in the Dominican Republic and in Mexico, and living together for nine months in Washington, DC—would have married. I had also been embraced fully by Ricky's family, and there were years of strong bonds that had formed between our respective family members, who were nevertheless oblivious, with the exception of my mother, to the very real issues between us, the two main characters in the drama. It was an unexpected and discomforting "divorce" for our families, even after we had each moved on.

Fernando and I settled down in a home in a diverse neighborhood in Silver Spring, Maryland, that we decorated elegantly and comfortably. He easily embraced my family and many friends, and I formed new relationships with his many visiting family members, and old and new friends. We entertained often, featuring his impressive cooking skills and mine, which are not too shabby either. I introduced my new husband to Washington, DC, including to some of the hidden gems that he might not have encountered despite his worldliness.

Fernando had little patience for the ignorant and insulting comments from some of my acquaintances. Some would not know where Angola was, or ask if he was referring to Angola, Louisiana, location of the notorious prison. We laughed for days over an acquaintance describing to him what a refrigerator was, assuming he didn't know.

Despite our happiness, however, I learned pretty early on that the experience of slavery in America and its long-enduring aftershocks created cultural rivers between some Africans and African Americans that can be challenging to ford. While many African Americans feel a genuine pride in our African roots, culturally there can be vast differences as well as uncanny centuries-old, shared customs between Africans and African Americans in behavior and expectations. My husband told me many times over my protestations, given my pride in my Afro-centrism, that I was shaped more by European than African culture. It angered me at the time, but in retrospect, I can understand that perspective.

I vividly recall a discussion the two of us had after he made the decision to move his two children, Lwena and Fernando, then ages eleven and fourteen, to the US. My husband had simply informed me, with no prior consultation or discussion, that they would soon be arriving to live with us. When I raised the practical implications and

From left: Panks, Fernando, and Lwena

challenges associated with this life change and suggested we discuss it, he reminded me that they were his blood, his children, and to be direct, that they were more important than I was. That, and many other expectations and patterns of behavior, made it clear to me that although generations of his family had known Africa as their home, and I come from ancestors who traversed the Middle Passage and were enslaved in America, he and I were truly from two very different worlds. I would have expected a decision that involved the health and welfare of the children, and the health and welfare of our marriage, to be an important enough marital discussion before any final decision was made. He did not.

Also, through my marriage, my travels to Africa, my work in the Caribbean, and my friends, I have observed a defining difference that informs each individual's cultural perspectives and personal conduct. Black people, and those who come from a majority culture, who are surrounded by a community and power structure that looks like them, carry themselves and interact in distinctly different ways from most African Americans. Our mangled history in America continues to cripple our perspective and sense of self. I remember the very moment I felt the rush of emotions when I looked around me in Haiti realizing that for the first time I was in a land of Black people; this was the first country to fight and win the battle for freedom in 1804, becoming the first independent Black nation. Despite the impoverishment of many citizens, the Haitian people carried themselves with an aura of confidence, pride, and comfort in their own skin. I believe this core difference is at the root of our often-complex relationships, both between us Black people, and with white Americans who often differentiate their perceptions of and interactions with Africans and Caribbean people, and often other immigrants of color, as distinct from their perceptions and interactions with African Americans. Curiously, some white Americans indicate that their interactions with Africans result in more favorable opinions and relationships than their interactions with their Black neighbors and colleagues. Conversely, I have found this to be true of African Americans and other communities of color in their interactions with the Diaspora, whether their origins are in a country that also experienced slavery or not. Whether they be Caribbean, from other countries with populations of color (even those with a slave narrative), or African, the deeply troubling distinctly US slave narrative continues to haunt our country.

Fernando told me that the best school near his hometown of Sanza Pombo, in Angola, was a Catholic boarding school run by Portuguese priests. He offered little in the way of detail, leading me to believe that any more elements of that experience would be too much for him to comfortably share. He did say that after that experience he had had enough of religion. Nevertheless, he occasionally went to the Shrine of the Immaculate Conception. His favorite day during Holy Week was Holy/ Maundy Thursday, commemorating when Jesus and the disciples celebrated the last supper. In some religious practices on that day, feet are washed during the service. Fernando liked the symbolism of it, the humility of washing a stranger's feet in church. I shared his love of the ritual, the simplicity and selflessness of the act. Helping raise my husband's Angolan children, Lwena and Panks (his son's nickname) and the birth of our daughter Briana were among the most rewarding experiences of my marriage.

The origin of the prefix "step" is eighth-century Latin-Old English meaning orphan. I've always considered it stigmatizing, maybe because "stepmother" has been portrayed that way in American culture. I will always consider them my son and older daughter. While "earned" may not be the right word, I feel deserving of the right to delete the "step" from all references to the two of them, given the years, realities, and their impressionable ages when our lives blended. My older children and I maintain a surprisingly close bond despite the challenges of distance now that they live in Angola and Mozambique, are married, and have families of their own. I was a major presence and influence in their lives when contact with their birth mother was limited by distance and circumstances. I was often the only parent visiting them at school or the lone parent at home when they were on breaks. Fernando, on several occasions, missing his daughter and wanting to ensure that all was well, would drive the 8 hours to visit for only a few hours with Lwena in boarding school. He travelled out of the country for extended periods in pursuit of oil projects, communicating to me the resolve that positive results were imminent. I sometimes wondered why the two children rarely appeared emotional when it was time for them to return to school. Over time, I came to realize that their lives had long been a series of major and minor adjustments to change. They had lived on

From left: Lwena, Panks, and Briana *(in front)*

three continents and in four countries by the time they were teenagers. They learned resilience and found ways to cope that I couldn't even imagine. I know they continue to feel my unconditional love, and they have been great siblings to my ever-amazing Briana, the daughter I share with Fernando.

When they joined our family unit, I found my older children, raised in Angola and Europe, to be courteous, obedient, and respectful. I have only two memories of conflict with them. Soon after graduating from high school, my son decided to drive to New York to visit a girlfriend. I regretted not having had "the talk" with him that every responsible American Black parent has with a Black child, particularly a son—the ritual explanation of what they should do if stopped by the police. To exacerbate the tension around this coming-of-age road trip, the girl's father was not a fan of the relationship. Nothing would stop Panks, however, so he learned several lessons the hard way. He was stopped by the police on a lonely road and made the mistake of stepping out of his car only to be confronted by the officer's drawn gun. Previously unfamiliar with the grave and often deadly consequences of such encounters for too many Black men in America, he was incredibly lucky to suffer only emotional bruises. He may have considered the encounter with the girl's father almost as intimidating.

Tangential to this incident, I also recall reprimanding him for an exorbitantly high long-distance phone bill (again with his girlfriend) that we could ill afford. This was the first conversation I had with Panks about the fact that I was now shouldering the family's bills and needed everyone's cooperation as we moved forward.

The incident that I recall with my older daughter remains a painful memory. For financial reasons, we transferred her to a public school for her last two years of high school. It was a major adjustment, and truly a culture shock for her not only because she is Angolan but also because she had previously attended a majority white boarding school. Unfortunately, the new school was quite an experience for her. She was not accepted by many of the African American students because of her unfamiliar behavior and refusal to adopt some of their cultural affinities and practices and in some cases, undesirable behavior. On one occasion, she dissolved into tears as she told us that we didn't appreciate that she wasn't on drugs or pregnant. As gently as we could, her father and I explained that we would never expect that she would be. We are still grateful for our neighbors, the Tignor family, the parents who became our friends, and their two lovely daughters, Kathy and April, Lwena's age, who became lifelong friends at the beginning of those difficult years of adjustment for my children.

Of my three children, only my son found a rapid and clear path to a new tribe in America. He shed his British accent almost overnight, adopted the cadence, vocabulary, and mannerisms of African American boys, and was rarely thought to be anything other than one of them. His US college friendships with his "boys" endure. My older daughter attended the American University of Paris (AUP) and has lasting friendships with an internation-

Lwena and Lauri, 2018

Pai holding Briana, 1992

al and multicultural circle. Both consider Angola home and remain comfortable professionally and personally in both cultures. Our close relationship has survived divorce from their father, distance and time. My youngest, a millennial, has made her home in Scotland over the last decade, since attending the University of Edinburgh.

In 1992, my husband and I had our only child together Briana Nsanga Fitz Pegado. There was so much that was different for her. She arrived at a time when her father was no longer positioned to provide her the full lifestyle afforded our two older children. Nevertheless, the silver lining of his years of frustration pursuing fruitless business ventures, was the time he was able to devote to Briana's care. Time was limited because of my work, and Pai (as he was called by his children) was an impactful presence in Briana's life in those early, formative years. I pulled more than my weight as the primary breadwinner, and Fernando became her principal caregiver. As a preschool child with a father at home to wrap around her tiny fingers, Briana and her father spent lots of time together at home, with Angolan friends and family, and at school events. Her father often joked that having her watch "Barney," the then popular big purple dinosaur

From left: Panks, his son David George, and AmGram ("American Grandma") Lauri, *courtesy of Fernando H. O. Pegado*

star of a children's television show, was his salvation. Schoolmates' parents hardly saw me during that time, but they all knew her father well.

Briana's doting brother, seventeen years her senior, provided her with loving attention and was generously present in her early life. Soon after she was born, when he was living on campus at the University of Maryland, he told us that he wanted to commute to campus from home so he could be more helpful with Briana when Fernando and I both needed to travel. His sacrifice strangely resulted in increasing his popularity with the girls, as he often took Briana to school and drew the pity of a young attractive teaching assistant who volunteered to properly comb Briana's hair. He also attracted attention from scores of young women on campus who admired him for toting his baby sister with him around campus. He certainly had plenty of practice for his role now as an attentive and loving father of three.

Briana's older sister Lwena, as a teenager transferring to Kennedy High School, around the corner from our home, for her last two years of high school cared for Briana after school. Our neighbors, the Tignor family girls, Kathy and April, were wonderful companions and friends for our children during their teenage years. Ernie Roane and his wife Evelyn were wonderful neighbors. I discovered that Michelle Wynn, our neighbor, and her husband Jim who lived around the corner, was a distant cousin (on the Mayes side of the family). The Tignors, along with my longtime assistant and friend, Pilar Martinez, rescued us, caring for baby Briana overnight on a couple of rare occasions. This circle of friends remains members of our extended family.

Briana was only eleven when her life changed dramatically, and her father and I separated. She was uprooted from her neighborhood friends and from our spacious home in the Maryland suburbs, and moved with me into a small urban apartment in DC. Most painful was the loss of time and attention from her father. Briana saw her father often until he returned to Angola around 2006, a few years after we separated, but the transition was difficult, confusing, and took an emotional toll on her.

After less than a year, Briana and I moved again to a larger place in DC recommended by my friend, Jill. It was a neighborhood with green space and parks near Briana's new school, and the neighborhood where school, church, and essentials for Briana were now within walking distance. Our new norm was slowly evolving.

We joined an Episcopal Church, St. Albans, with a vibrant youth program, where Briana developed friendships and mentors. I am forever grateful to Toby Moffett and his wife, Myra, for their support during this difficult period. Toby and Myra always invited us to family holiday celebrations at their home. I shared office space with Toby, some clients, and the support of his ever-competent multitalented assistant, Jackie Harrell.

The Moffetts had recommended St. Albans where they were parishioners. Briana attended Grace Episcopal Day School for a few years, after a difficult transition

Lauri and Briana, circa 2002

from a stable family life in the suburbs to just the two of us living in apartments in the city, and although it did not have the diverse congregation that I would have preferred for us, Briana was immediately very comfortable with her new friends there. She embraced the many laudable experiences afforded the kids there, including grate patrol (preparing food and delivering it into the hands of the homeless on the streets of Washington, DC), building and repairing homes in Appalachia, and walking many miles on the Camino de Santiago, the famous pilgrimage in northern Spain. While I had grown up in the Episcopal Church, and in my mother's AME Church when I was with my maternal grandparents in North Brentwood, Maryland, Briana was baptized a Catholic in Lisbon with her Angolan grandmother, father, and family members. Work precluded me from going on that important trip.

Always exuding a strong and confident personality, by seventh grade Briana and her two best friends from middle school, Natalie Joslin and Hanna Wade, attended music classes after school and formed a rock band, "Syndrome." They were surprisingly good, competed in

Briana, *photographer Matt Beech*

several "Battle of the Bands" contests and performed on occasion at local venues. The three of them were also good soccer players, coached by David Joslin, Natalie's father. A further indication of Briana's unique path, in which she fought against being typecast and avoided easy labeling, was that she tried out for and played on the boys' football team and wore only black clothing and black fingernail polish long before it became a fashion trend. She continues to make her mark and is understated about her many firsts: being elected president of one of the largest student unions in Scotland at the University of Edinburgh; serving on the boards of cutting-edge women's organizations and nonprofits; advocating vociferously for equity and inclusion for all humans, particularly artists; revolutionizing the creative sector in Edinburgh; saving our planet from environmental destruction and human apathy; and educating and addressing—through her extensive exposure in the print, broadcast, and social media—bias and discrimination regarding race, gender, self-identification, body shaming, and physical and mental abuse. I am proud of Briana, and supportive of her independent path as she grows into her comfort zone. She voraciously embraces issues of culture, art, sustainability, and the evolution of thought about innovation and technology.

My husband had been very generous financially to his family of fourteen living siblings until he lost the income and reputation of his London-based high-ranking prestigious position at an Angolan state-owned energy company. His youngest sister Minga grew up as something of a daughter to him and sibling to his two children. He had become embroiled in allegations of financial mismanagement at the time we were married in 1988, from which he would only emerge over ten years later, and that would take a major toll—reputational, financial, health, and emotional—on him and on us as a couple. A few years into our marriage, it became my anxiety-producing responsibility to support our family's established lifestyle. We both dealt with unexpected consequences—he developed diabetes and I, high blood pressure. Although other work options and opportunities presented themselves, my husband never managed to find any of them acceptable to him. Instead of recapturing the life of an achieving, financially stable, gainfully employed man, he became the "Man of la Mancha," chasing a costly dream of the next "big deal."

That endless pursuit required long and costly trips across the ocean. As he accumulated extensive debt, individuals from whom he had borrowed money placed harassing calls to me to seek payment. This difficult and unhealthy environment became untenable for both of us, and we painfully separated and subsequently divorced. After we separated, he found it even more difficult to live in the US and eventually returned to Angola. He lived his last decade in the country of his birth, close to his supportive family, but never relinquishing his chase for the unreachable dream. His health challenges and the stress of that quest led to his passing in the summer of 2020, hopefully crossing over to a place of mental and physical peace. I watched the burial in Luanda on Zoom—two children sobbing behind their face masks soaked in the tears streaming from their weary eyes as they took their turn shoveling the dirt to cover the casket lowered into the hole containing his remains, but never his spirit. Simultaneously, I could see on another square on my screen the unmasked face and eyes of his "filha querida," beloved daughter Briana Nsanga, who was watching the burial of her father from her living room in Edinburgh. The masks required during the COVID-19 pandemic could not hide our eyes, the windows to the soul.

Fernando and I had good years together over our fifteen-year marriage, and I wanted to believe his promises about the one or other deal that might finally come through. I had fallen into a trap of optimism until the moment I finally accepted that his plan wasn't working and indeed never would if he continued down the same road. I tried, but there was no way to get him to understand that without a change, our marriage would be the one partnership that would surely implode.

The separation and divorce catapulted me into the ranks of single Black mothers and of sole support for my daughter and me. "You can do bad by yourself," the often-heard adage in the Black community reminded me. I heard the words in my head and did everything I could to keep the two of us moving forward. Although I was in that income bracket that was not eligible for financial support from her private schools, and I was making ends meet, my daughter and I would be subjected to the stigma and assumptions associated with single Black motherhood in our society. Throughout my life, I had suffered from the "accusation" that my success was unearned, and that my performance was judged by a lower standard because of my race and gender. Ironically, I believed the opposite and worked to the utmost to ensure that, if anyone bothered to objectively observe, the record would inevitably reflect the fact that I would "always work twice as hard to receive half the credit."

I enjoy being "AmGram" (American Grandma) to my five grandchildren. My older children never have judged me nor questioned why I divorced their father. Their well-earned success at American companies in one field of expertise and their father's industry, fossil fuels, has met with great disapproval from my youngest, who reminds all of us openly and often of her deeply held and passionate opinions that our many transgressions are contributing to the demise of the planet.

I have come to believe that in the later years of my marriage, once I recognized the futility of trying to repair what was irreparably broken, that I continued to stay put due to a variety of factors, including a fear of failure; ingrained discipline from my upbringing and years in ballet; a high tolerance for emotional and physical pain; my determination and persistence; and my ability to overcome adversity. I know some of the reasons, of course, were tied up with our children, my husband's health, our deep love for, and responsibility to, our family, and the plane crash in Croatia, in April 1996, when Briana was three. Panks was at home alone with Briana fielding innumerable calls from friends and family desperate to find out if I was on that plane.

I recall then and now that Ron had liked Fernando, and despite what I had shared with him about the chaos in our marriage, he had encouraged me to stay with him.

CHAPTER SEVEN

Dancing to the Drumbeat

We share the same parents, but Bruce, the older of my two brothers identifies as Native American; he gave up considering himself African American a very long time ago. His choice likely stems from his internalized distress of the many experiences of discrimination and abuse suffered by so many African Americans in this country, and the realization that being Black holds limited joy for him. Maybe men in my family are so pained by what they know to be the continuing plight of Black men, who suffer disproportionately higher incarceration rates in America's prisons, are more likely to be unemployed, and are more likely to be pulled over by the police and even shot. Although they may be born into strong, upstanding Black families, each is only one step away from any and every cursed fate. As I watched my brother grow into manhood in a place that more often undermines rather than honors him, I always have known that it was not easy for him—or for other men in my family to live as Black men in this country. It is likely that these lived experiences, more often painful and unspoken, have forced many of them to dance to the beat of a different drum.

My brother believes that it is not coincidental that his given name is Bruce, which means "from the thicket." He has always, as have other Native Americans, identified closely with nature and the wilderness. Most often, he is unflappable, calm, tranquil, and comfortable with his solitude—characteristics associated with Native Americans. When he and kids in the neighborhood played cowboys and Indians, he quickly elected to be an Indian. When little boys became obsessed with the action figure GI Joe, Bruce idolized his Chief Cherokee action figure. He played with Chief Cherokee and his horse for hours on end and fell asleep with him under his bed covers. He has studied the complex history of Native Americans, and we have discussed the narrative of their struggle with colonialists to keep the land; disease and violence at the hands of European colonialists and immigrants; the Trail of Tears displacing them from their land; suffering the stripping of their culture to accept Christianity; providing refuge to fleeing slaves; enslaving Africans; refusing to accept Blacks as enfranchised members of their communities who share their heritage, culture, and genes.

Recognizing my brother's choice to identify with this part of his heritage, I have made it my practice to give him many gifts crafted by or depicting Native Americans. He proudly displays them, along with a unique onyx table with Aztec images I bought in Mexico during my diplomatic tour and that he always admired. I finally gave him the table as a centerpiece in his sparsely decorated apartment. His minimalist environment and selective appointment of furniture and art create an atmosphere both isolated and tranquil; it is his refuge.

While Bruce, at such a young age, didn't know any of his family background and only heard snippets about it when he was much older, the Native American blood running through his veins must have given voice to his ancestors whose spirits spoke to him. He has said that he did not choose this identity, but that it chose him.

When I was a young girl, I accompanied my paternal Grandma to her family reunion and pow-wow with her relatives, who were members of the Saponi/Haliwa tribe in Hollister, North Carolina. Bruce told me that he went with Grandma on another occasion to Hollister to meet an elder of the tribe in search of documents related to land owned by her Native American Grandpa Keen, who my father has often mentioned with pride and affection.

Beyond a few such brief stories, there was little talk about our family history, on either my father's or mother's side of the family. Many subjects in African American homes, including our genealogy and familial connections, are cloaked in secrecy, and are seldom discussed inside the walls of the home—and never outside. I was taught from childhood to keep my business under lock and key, and not to share personal information with others. I have wondered whether this practice originated from the survival instincts of our enslaved ancestors—in protecting their families and communities from their masters, using creative truths, pretense, secrets, signals, and a language all their own.

My father recently gave me a detailed, written account that, thankfully, fills in many of the gaps in what Bruce and I were able to surmise as we compared notes; it also sheds light on why my paternal grandparents avoided a complete and factual accounting of our family history, and sometimes became agitated at our queries, or were reticent when questioned about the family.

At one point, Bruce, who my mother described as "never missing a trick," observed that my paternal grandmother's driver's license described her race as "white." As young children will do, he asked her why. She responded in an irritated tone, "Bruce, that is what they put on my license when I first got it." I always thought that she must have had ample opportunity to change it on numerous occasions when it was renewed, and yet she had not. I imagine that a reason she didn't is that it proved advantageous on occasion in the little southern town of Warrenton, North Carolina, and in places farther afield.

According to my father, his mother, Irene Hawkins, was a child born to a mixed Native American and white mother Madgie Keen, and a white father Charles Hawkins, believed to be English. Madgie and Charles Hawkins had seven children, including Grandma Irene, before they divorced. My great-grandmother, Madgie, had been the only child of Norman Long Keen (after whom my father was named), a successful grocery store owner in Hollister and scion of the Saponi Indian tribe, and his wife Virginia Hall, a white woman from Ahoskie, North Carolina. Keen was born in the 1860s and was from the Ahoskie area that was, at that time, almost exclusively Native American and white. Given the environment at the time, those of white/Indian lineage in Hollister were known to disassociate their heritage from that of the descendants of enslaved Africans. History indicates that interracial marriages between those two races were quite common. The Keens had moved to Hollister to start their married life there.

Grandpa Keen, my father's great-grandfather and his wife were accepted fully in that community, where he owned and operated a general store that catered to the farmers in the area. The store supplied the basics of what they needed for life on their farms: seeds for crops, fertilizer, and equipment. In addition, the store sold flour, meal, baking and cooking goods, and utensils.

My grandfather, Charles Steel Fitz, who eventually ran that grocery store in Hollister, was from Warrenton, a true "Old South" town and a bastion of the slave tradition. Dad's paternal grandfather, Philip Fitz (after whom

Dad's brother was named), was the offspring of his German slave master. Philip was married to Hattie Burgess who was the progeny of a slave master and a Native American from the Warrenton slave market (some Native Americans were also enslaved, and history tells us that many Africans fleeing slavery were sheltered at Indian reservations). Charles, my grandfather, was one of Philip and Hattie's seven children. Although he was light skinned, too, Charles was darker than his "high yaller" wife, my Grandma Irene, and he was considered colored or Negro. Bruce reminded me about our grandfather's ritual application of Dr. Freddie Palmer's bleaching cream, and that when he slept, whether at night or even during his customary afternoon nap, a trusty stocking cap made from his wife's nylons was always on his head to ensure his hair stayed smoother and straighter.

Choosing Irene from the insular Hollister community to be his wife faced opposition from both her family and the community at large. Bold and determined, he persevered and won her over, thereby defying her family. They eloped and fled the South, escaping to Harlem, New York, where many southern Blacks and whites suffering from the failing economy and the approaching depression sought a better life (the Great Migration). Irene was

Maternal great-grandfather
Charles Hawkins

Norman and Philip, circa 1940

From left, back row: Grandaddy Fitz, Great-great-grandpa Keen, Great Uncle Basil; *front row:* Philip and Norman

sixteen years old when she gave birth to her first child, a son Philip, soon after migrating north; my father was born thirteen months later. Some of her Hawkins clan and several of Charles' siblings also had moved to New York City before Charles and Irene began their new life together there.

My grandfather Charlie, as he was called, had an eighth-grade education, and my grandmother not much more. He became a doorman at the Ritz-Carlton Hotel and Grandma, due to her fair complexion, was hired as a coffeehouse counter girl. Their maternal grandmother Madgie, who they named "Two-Mamas" (they considered her a second mother as opposed to a grandmother), cared for Dad and Philip. It was at this time that Charles, sensitized by his own unacceptance by the Hawkins family, recognized the different and better treatment Philip was afforded by his wife's Hollister family members and tried on weekends for both his sons, Philip and Norman (especially Norman, given the limited attention he received in comparison to his brother) to visit Charles' siblings in New York: Big Shadrick (Shad), Little Shad, Eva, and Gertrude. Aunt Gert showered Dad with love and affection until her death. As a young child living in New York, I was a witness to my dad and Aunt Gert's special relationship.

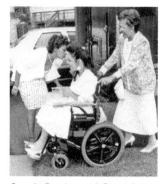

Cousin Denise and Great Aunt Lee, *1988, photographer Milton Williams*

Lauri. *Painting by Denise Hawkins, circa 1970, photographer Edward C. Jones*

She became Bruce's godmother.

I can still picture the New York family members on both sides—Two-Mammas, Aunt Clay, Uncle Clarence (with whom we lived for a while, along with his wife Rita, and their children), Aunt Saluda, who had mental health issues and lived with us at our Southeast Washington, DC, home for a while, and Uncle Basil, who with his wife, the lively Aunt Lee, had four children. Three of the four were wheelchair bound with muscular dystrophy. Diane was the only one who escaped the debilitating disease. I particularly liked to visit and play games with the youngest, Denise (Niecy), who was always attentive and so nice to me. I treasure her painting of me, done before use of her hands became limited. I often reflect on the full life of travel and joy their parents provided their three children when modern equipment, medicines, and therapy were as yet undiscovered or unavailable. I also consider the toll it must have taken on Diane.

Back in Hollister in the late 1930s, Grandpa Keen was approaching his eightieth birthday and needed help running his general store business. All his family had moved north, and with the onset of World War II, many of the men in the family were drafted, and he was left with few options. He selected Grandaddy Charlie Fitz to save the Keen/Hawkins family store. Grandma Irene Fitz had always been a favorite of her Grandpa Keen, and she was delighted to move the family back to Hollister. With hard work, determination, and perseverance, Grandaddy Fitz succeeded in learning the business and becoming highly successful despite the racism and jealousy the community showed toward him.

Charlie Fitz had expanded the store by adding and installing several booths to serve food and drinks (mostly beer and wine) and purchased a "piccolo" (jukebox) that played blues and all the popular music of the day. It became the place to go on Friday nights and weekends for fun and entertainment. As one might expect, some of the farmers occasionally would have too much to drink and become rowdy. The sheriff was sometimes called and would either reluctantly arrive or not come at all. One night when one of the farmers became drunk and threatening, Grandaddy had to force him out of the store. In the next half hour, the man returned, still inebriated and staggering, but now waving a switchblade and charging at my grandfather. As the man lunged at him, Grandaddy reached for his 45 revolver under the counter and fired one shot. The bullet hit the man right between the eyes and he died in a pool of blood on the floor.

That my grandfather was acquitted for murder at a hearing of the local tribunal, and that the shooting was considered self-defense, was unusual for the times and fortuitous. A few weeks later, however, the victim's male relatives tricked Grandaddy into coming out of his home to meet a nonexistent visitor. They took revenge by beating my grandfather to within an inch of his life on his own front lawn. He was also stabbed repeatedly and left bleeding on the ground. My grandmother was able to get him to the hospital in Rocky Mount, twenty-eight miles away, in time for the doctors to save him after patching his shredded back with dozens of stitches.

This was not the only trauma to reverberate from that incident. My father was marked forever because he and his brother, both teenagers at the time, had witnessed it all. They had seen my grandfather shoot and kill a man in self-defense. They had seen the drunken man who dared to attack him become the unfortunate victim who would "take a bullet" for the jealous and racist community in which they lived. It was a lot for two young boys to manage, and it then quickly became entwined with yet another painful event in our family's history; soon after the incident, Grandpa Keen died, and Charles Fitz sent his family to his mother in Warrenton, North Carolina, and closed the store.

We never knew what ghosts haunted my grandfather later in life, or what might have led him to accidentally shoot himself, resulting in the loss of an eye. As he aged and spent more time resting in bed, he often summoned my mother alone to sit with him when we visited. He loved talking to the daughter-in-law he lovingly, and in his Southern drawl called, "Jahwce." He would lie in his bed and talk as she listened. When he died, she was the one who, at his request, had written down every detail for his funeral that he outlined so meticulously during those conversations. Perhaps he confessed to her what really happened during that evening many years earlier in his store. Maybe she had learned why a man who was an expert with a firearm could shoot out his own eye while cleaning his gun. We will never know; my mother was the best keeper of secrets I have ever known. She emanated her trustworthiness and unwillingness to judge others, creating a safe space for people to unload. As many times as I have found myself the recipient of trusted information that I never share with others, I know I must have inherited that gift from her.

Fitz family in North Carolina, 1917

I have so many sweet memories from my childhood of visiting my grandparents during many summers spent in Warrenton, North Carolina. The country store they owned, Fitz Grocery, was in the Black section of town. My grandfather's brother also owned his own business, a car repair garage, Fitts Garage, in the neighboring town of Henderson. I have only recently learned a believable explanation for the different spellings of their last name.

According to my father, early in the 1920s before the great Depression, several of my great-grandfather Philip Fitts' siblings fled the south and moved north to One, Shadrick Fitts was the first to change his name to Fitz, perhaps to signal his new life in the north, and to mark his escape from the racist "Old South." Grandpa Fitts, embracing his new life, emulated his Great Uncle Shad and changed the spelling of his name to "Fitz" while some of his brothers who remained in North Carolina kept the original spelling. Throughout my life, when the subject arose, we were told a variety of stories about why blood brothers spelled their last names differently. I have come to understand this is one more way in which the men in our family danced to the beat of their own drum.

Brother Neal, circa 2012

My brother Bruce and I reminisced about those summers in Warrenton with our grandparents and Aunts Jeanine and Diane, my father's much younger sisters. We regret that our younger brother, Neal, who was born eight years after Bruce, never experienced those formative days.

My grandmother taught me how to make sandwiches for customers at the Fitz Grocery lunch counter, and in the back, we were taught how to season and steam the pulled pork. I prepared the barbecue sandwiches and wieners with chili or sauerkraut and came to understand what customer service is—how to treat people, how to smile through the pain, and to appear pleasant and always welcoming—and through it all, we knew to add just the right amount of Southern hospitality. At "the house" I learned to cook, to can fruits and vegetables, to make jelly and jam, churn ice cream, hang clothes to dry in the sun, slip away to visit the sick, to manage to fit into one day what should have been achieved over three, and to gossip playfully about people. From my grandfather, I learned precision, process, and the right way to do things, which meant, of course, doing things his way. I remember stocking the shelves, weighing, and packaging the fresh fish, meat, and fresh vegetables. We also pumped gas, counted the money we returned to customers, or as they called it, "making change," kept records of customer debt, and closed out the cash register at day's end. Grandpa Fitz loved music, recited poetry, and had a beautiful voice. Many nights he recited dramatic poems such as Edgar Allen Poe's "The Raven," with

Mom reciting with him the long verses ending in the poem's haunting refrain, "quoth the Raven 'Nevermore." As a child, I was fascinated by the rhythmic voices of the duet, Grandaddy Fitz and Mom. The meaning of the words was secondary and likely beyond my comprehension anyway. I heard the question asked of the Raven, whether there is "balm in Gilead" and only years later understood the biblical origin of the reference, Jeremiah, 8–22:

Is there no balm in Gilead?
Is there no physician there?
Why then is there no healing
for the wounds of my people.

It amazed me that it was customary for my older relatives to have memorized these epic poems. This practice reflects a heritage of valuing the oral tradition and the importance of storytelling. On other nights, before our bedtime, Grandaddy Fitz pulled out his zither, playing and singing melodies we grew to love. My father likely inherited his acting talent from his father. And, from both of my grandparents, I learned the importance of community, traditions, hard work, spontaneous adventures, faith, music, laughter, and survival.

I recall the fear of riding the bus with my brother Bruce from Washington, DC, to Warrenton, North Carolina, and seeing the "Colored" water fountains and the "Whites Only" signs at the rest stops where the bus stopped for riders to get food and use the restrooms. In Warrenton, with my Black friends, we were restricted to the balcony of the movie theater while white people sat downstairs. I admit to dropping a few popcorn kernels off that balcony onto those below, although I do think it must have been by accident, of course. One night in 1964, in an act of defiance, my parents dared to sit downstairs to see the movie, A *Hard Day's Night*, about the rock group, the Beatles. I had also heard the account of my Uncle Ronald being reprimanded by the owner of a "whites only" laundromat next door to Fitz Grocery, who took umbrage at a Negro using his "Whites Only" facilities, and thereby failing to obey the rules of his establishment. Imagine the look of consternation on the face of the white proprietor, when my uncle, feigning a look of surprise, responded, "But I only put white clothes in your washing machine."

On Sundays, we attended All Saints Episcopal Church with our grandparents. It had an all-Negro congregation and was only blocks away from the whites only Episcopal Church. A white B&B owner recently told me that the Black All Saints Church housed in its basement a school for mixed race children of enslaved women who otherwise could not attend school. My grandfather was a deacon at All Saints, which remains a Black church in the hometown of one of the early Black Bishop missionaries. Suffragan (the limited status Black bishops were allowed at the time) Bishop Bravid Washington Harris, a paternal relative, was among the first African American missionaries to Sub-Saharan Africa, and his legacy in Liberia has added to the rich history of the relationships between Africans and African Americans. Karen Cox, my treasured Liberian Vassar alumna and friend who has been so instrumental and indispensable to my writing this memoir about my journey, told me that the school in Monrovia named for him, the B.W. Harris High School, continues in operation in Monrovia, Liberia. The school counts educators, lawyers, and physicians among its many successful graduates.

Presiding Bishop Michael Curry, whom I had met at a Council on Foreign Relations breakfast where he was a speaker, is the first African American presiding bishop and primate of the Episcopal Church. He and my paternal family share a connection to North Carolina where he was previously a bishop of the diocese of North Carolina. My family has a long history in the North Carolina Episcopal Church, and I am a "cradle" Episcopalian. Given my paternal family's long history in the Episcopal Church and my familiarity with Black Episcopalians, I was disappointed to learn that the church in the US is 98 percent white.

It was Bishop Curry who, in his customary impassioned style, delivered the sermon—shocking to the uninitiated; met by squirming and looks of disapproval by some of the nobility and gentry; and uplifting and inspiring for many of us—at the royal wedding of Prince Harry and Megan Markle. We all experience random events that evoke unanticipated reactions in us. So, while many reasons drew viewers to watch the wedding of Megan Markle to Prince Harry, I was uncharacteristically emotional as I took it all in, from the first moments to the last. To some, it may have appeared a mere meeting of a fairy tale with a reality show. For me, it generated a constant flow of tears because of its historical significance and personal relevance. I found the most poignant scene to be that of the elegant mother of the bride, unaccompanied, sitting in the Church pew, radiating an aura of quiet dignity, class, humility, and pride, exceeding that of all the royals and celebrities assembled. As the tears rolled down my cheeks, I thought of my daughter Briana living in Scotland. I shared another Black mother's solitude, quiet defiance, and victory over the many odds confronting us and many other single Black mothers and their daughters.

Recently, my dear friend Liz Joslin (the mother of a member of my younger daughter's all-girl rock band in middle school) and I decided to take a Thelma and

Louise-style journey to Asheville, North Carolina. We planned an idyllic drive through Virginia into North Carolina to see the wondrous, world-renowned glass art of Dale Chihuly on exhibit at the Biltmore Estate.

I suggested my family's hometown of Warrenton as our overnight rest stop in route to Asheville. We enjoyed a far–too-infrequent dinner with my father's remaining youngest sister Aunt Diane (his other sister Jeanine passed some years earlier) and her husband Clarence Lee, a central character in my Warrenton coming-of-age circle of friends. We also visited my father's cousin, Hermenia (Fitts) Salmon, daughter of the great uncle who owned Fitts Garage, and her husband Harold. While both are advanced in age, Hermenia's memory is as clear as a bell, and we stayed much longer than anticipated listening to stories about her youth, life in New York City, and marriage to Harold. We spent the night at a B&B on a block in a part of town that I dared not traverse as a child. At the end of the block, on the corner, is the former whites only high school that my childhood friends integrated in the 1960s while I was integrating schools in Montgomery County, Maryland. Coincidentally, Liz and I attended the same high school, but did not become friends until our daughters, Natalie and Briana, became friends at school on stage and on the soccer field. I marveled at how little had changed as we drove past the two Episcopal churches that even today largely remain segregated, along with the funeral parlors that are divided, even in matters of dying, along racial lines. Strange as it is, we are fairly certain the dearly departed had cared deeply enough about their "homegoing," that they ensured their remains were laid to rest under the same circumstances in which they had lived their lives.

Over breakfast, we listened to stories shared by the white owner of the B&B about a meeting of the Confederate generals that took place in Warrenton. Warrenton was one of the wealthiest towns in the state of North Carolina from 1840 to 1860; it was also the trading center of an area of rich tobacco and cotton plantations and historic architecture. My friend, who is white, also commented on the continuing social separation and marginalization of Black people in the town.

As a relevant side note to the experience Liz and I had traveling through the South, my friend Sharon Freeman, and I were enlightened by our mutual friend, Sandra Taylor, on a misconception regarding race, segregation, and the South. During one of our many delightfully animated, wide-ranging, and candid conversations, we learned that though we grew up around the same time, Sandra's experience differed from being raised in a Black working-class neighborhood in Birmingham, Alabama, where the community lived well, and protected and insulated their children from the pain of the Jim Crow system. As a result, Sandra experienced little discrimination in the protective bubble her family and community created. Even growing up at the same time and place of the tragic 16th Street Baptist Church bombing of 1963, Sandra shared another reality lived by some of my generation of children in the South. I had always imagined that daily life for the three of us, as close in age as we are, was largely a shared experience of micro- and macro-aggressions from the majority community. But Sandra's early life had been somewhat different. She lived in an African American community of safety and security in Birmingham, Alabama, where families were comfortable remaining in their familiar environments, where they patronized their traditional stores, and attended their family churches.

Desegregation continues to encounter this reality where "separate but equal" is the preferred lifestyle for some. "Integration" has been replaced with equity and inclusion, and more recently, gentrification brings modern challenges to old, never-resolved problems. With that conversation, one of many I enjoy with my circle of "sistah friends," I better understood a presentation at the Aspen Institute by famed African American photographer Dawoud Bey about his research for a powerful exhibit about that 1963 Church bombing. Bey brilliantly juxtaposed a current photograph of a child the age of one of the victims beside an adult of the age that child would be today, had she or he not lost their life to senseless violence. Bey was advised to expect it to be difficult or even impossible to speak with, not to mention photograph, relatives of those young victims of the bombing. While this proved to be true, he did learn of the mental distress and resulting dysfunction experienced by some of the survivors and relatives of those lost in the violence. None of those pictured in the exhibition knew each other, nor were they photographed at the same session. Nonetheless, the brilliant matching of the photographs laid bare an eerie resemblance between the subjects. Today, despite its historical significance in the history of the nation, neither the City of Birmingham nor the State of Alabama have erected even one statue or historical marker to honor those killed in the bombing of the 16th Street Baptist Church.

Sharon is from Philadelphia, and I am from Washington, DC. Sharon and I met in our professional capacity in the trade area, and I am always astounded by her novel ideas and the subjects of whatever would become her next book. She has an uncanny way of writing her dozens of books on wide-ranging subjects from business to baseball. If she is not well versed in the subject, she expertly researches, conducts interviews, and acquires the requisite knowledge. Sandra and I had met in Mexico City when we were both in the Foreign Service and were friends through our many subsequent professional journeys—mine in the public and private sectors, hers as a senior executive at Kodak and Starbucks and directing a trade association, and later as we sat on corporate and nonprofit boards. Sandra has been a professor and is on track to distinguish herself in the world of wine, writing and speaking about sustainable wines after earning an M.B.A. at the Bordeaux School of Management/Kedge Business School in France. We three Black women share the education, professional experience as well as exposure to countries around the globe, the desire to take calculated risks, and a spirit of adventure. We are able to reinvent ourselves and delight in the journey.

Long drives south like the one Liz and I had embarked on seem always to have been part of my life. When we lived in New York, the ride was usually to Maryland or North Carolina. Mom would always pack a delicious lunch and surprise snacks that we loved, maybe cherries—our favorite fruit—or a pastry with a cherry on top. My parents were always good at saving money, so I know that was part of the reason for the packed meals, but so was not having to stop for a bathroom (also the reason for the empty cylindrical tennis ball cans), or to find food in an unwelcoming town. On the way south, we often rode through Dinwiddie in Virginia; when we arrived there, Dad would always say, "Dinwiddie—it ain't no town and it ain't no city." Eventually, every time the exits to Dinwiddie came into view, my mother, Bruce, or I would chant the same refrain, even before Dad teed it up for us.

There was another family favorite that we stumbled upon during a memorable drive south to the Nationals in New Orleans, a Black tennis tournament where Dad was a regular competitor. I was in college and had been driving for several years, and my mom was not particularly fond of highway driving, so I was always the one who gave Dad a break at the wheel. But somewhere in the South, I exceeded the speed limit, apparently having inherited my father's racing car driver alter ego, and a police officer pulled us over. He was a dead ringer for the Rod Steiger character from the movie starring Sydney Poitier, *In the Heat of the Night*. I must have been speeding so I was truly nervous but having heard "the talk" that Black and Brown parents have had to give far too many times about what to do if stopped by the police, I knew to just sit there sweating. The police officer exited his car and swaggered over to the driver's window, peering into the car past me to see my father in the front passenger seat and my mother and brothers in the back. His eyes landed on me and he said, "You were driving kinda fast. Above the speed limit. Let me see your driver's license and registration." While I responded to his request, my father apologized, explaining, "Sorry, Officer. It's my daughter driving." The Officer came back with an "Oh, Lord," that rolled out in the deepest Southern drawl imaginable and that sounded to our ears like "Aaarh Lawd." Dad went on to explain that I had recently gotten my driver's license and was giving him a break on our long drive to New Orleans. As my dad turned on the charm to convince the Officer not to issue me a ticket, every few words he uttered were met by an "Aaarh Lawd" from the Officer. After he let us go with a warning (thankfully!), we laughed in relief and repeated that phrase which we instantly adopted as our family's favorite expression of comic relief from that day forward.

On our road trip, Liz and I drove past the now-abandoned shell that once was my grandfather's country store, a place that had literally been assembled by the hands of my father and uncle. Locked behind its crumbling exterior, I could still feel the vibrancy of the activity around that sandwich counter where I had loved to mix the pulled pork barbecue in the steamer and to line up buns to make sandwich after sandwich. This was where I had first learned to operate a cash register, to slice and weigh the baloney, and to smile broadly at every customer as

Shell of Fitz Grocery, 2018

I imitated my Grandma Fitz's Southern drawl, "How do, how you?" I took pictures that day and, encouraged by Liz, decided to go to the county courthouse to find the real estate records associated with the property. Later, I spent days thinking about how to purchase and restore that family treasure, to honor the community legacy it represented. I even asked a dear and unforgettable child-hood friend who became a local sheriff, Durwood Wright, and who knew the current owner, to contact him about the property. It is still a well-located piece of real estate and remains the place that had engendered so many memories and so much history for my family and for the town. I know that there are many abandoned build-ings like this one in Black neighborhoods throughout the South with similar stories trapped inside of falling walls, boarded up windows, and creaking floorboards. I know there are many of us who, just like me, would be enveloped by memories of long-gone times, and searing experiences that mark critical stages in America's his-tory. We are often overwhelmed by the emotional and physical scars of painful lives lived and left, that never completely heal, but that add dimension to our hearts and souls and that helped build our strong characters. We recall the joy and the pain of living in an America alternating between denial of its long difficult racial history and openly hostile expressions of anger and hate that bubble up from its underbelly.

Liz and I continued to Asheville, North Carolina, to the Dale Chihuly exhibit, the famous intricate glass sculptures, displayed at the Vanderbilt family's Biltmore Estate, and observed how segregated the city remains. I was the only, or among the very few, people of color we saw at any of the places we visited over those three days; Black people were not at the hotel, or at the exhibit, or at any of the restaurants where we dined. Later, Liz recalled the looks and even comments of surprise expressed by some proprietors as we shopped. I hardly took note of any of them as I had experienced such behavior before, too many times to count.

Upon our arrival in Asheville, I called my Aunt Julie, my father's brother, Uncle Philip's, second wife. They were divorced several decades ago, and she lives with their son, my cousin Michael, in a house tucked into the side of the Black Mountain range of Asheville. It was a visit with once-close relatives I had not seen for many years; the conversation was peppered with both laughter and sadness. Ironically, I have always thought my friend and traveling companion, Liz, had a striking resemblance to my Aunt Julie. Of course, I had never mentioned it to her given that I could not have imagined the two of them would ever be in the same room. We reminisced and told family stories, which we all agreed, you "couldn't make up, if you tried."

Aunt Julie and Uncle Phil married after meeting at University in Indiana where their life-changing journey began. They both were from North Carolina. She was engaged to a man in Asheville, and Uncle Phil had a wife and two young daughters in Warrenton. Their romance was quite a scandal in the late 1950s. (Interracial marriage in all US states did not become fully legal until the 1967 Supreme Court's *Loving v. Virginia* ruling.) When falling in love disrupted theirs and many others' lives, defied State laws, and the bounds of acceptable racial behavior (she was, after all, a white woman), Uncle Philip was soon chased out of North Carolina by the Ku Klux Klan (KKK).

Running as far as he could, my uncle put five hundred miles between himself and his old life, divorced the mother of his two daughters, and put down roots in New York with Aunt Julie, where their two sons were born and where they had lived for many years. On the day of our visit, my aunt—who had been very close to my mother, as they shared a teaching profession, love of literature, and similar warm and perceptive personalities—told me a few of her vivid memories of the time. We laughed hard recounting stories about visits to their home, when it was so apparent that she and her sons, my white aunt and biracial cousins, were comfortable with, and accepting of me and their other brown family members—while, sadly, my "blood uncle," a Black man by society's standards, was not. When I was in undergraduate school in Poughkeepsie, New York, my dad suggested that instead of returning home to DC, I spend the school break with my uncle and family in Long Island, N.Y. One day, I overheard my Uncle Phil and Aunt Julie talking about the evening commitment the family had made to attend a wrestling match that my cousins were participating in, and for which my Uncle was the coach. Uncle Phil was lamenting what they should do with me that evening since they couldn't have me accompany them to the match. "How would she be introduced?" he asked. Aunt Julie replied, "Well, of course she'll go, and I will introduce her as my niece."

Aunt Julie, with her quiet Southern charm, was a woman before her time. Her lifelong best friend is a Black woman, and she was always accepting and matter of fact about her biracial family. When both their and our fami-

From left: Cousins Chris and Michael Fitz and brother Bruce

lies lived in New York and Uncle Phil and family visited us at our apartment, my young cousins Michael and Christopher, who were about the same age as my brother Bruce, interrupted their play and like innocent and inquisitive children, one asked his mother right on the spot, why his cousin Bruce was brown, and he was white. I will never forget Aunt Julie's simple and patient response. In her lilting Southern drawl, she responded, "You see those freckles on your face? Well, Bruce had so many freckles that they bunched together and formed one big freckle that covers his whole body."

Although we were very young and didn't know it at the time, my uncle had chosen to "pass," to live his life as a white man at a time when work, and everything else, was significantly more difficult for those of us with darker hues. So here I found myself speaking with a white woman about visits to her home, while her Black but passing husband, my uncle, had been more concerned than she about being seen with and associating with us, his Black relatives.

My Uncle Phil's first wife was a beautiful Black woman. I once saw a picture of her and my mother in their twenties. They were sure to stop traffic. My uncle and his first wife have two daughters who are around my age. I remember them fondly from our youth, and my grand-

Great-grandma "Two Mamas"
with cousins Toni, Cheri, and Lauri

mother mentioned them every time I visited in the summers. I discovered many years ago that one of them had settled in Washington, DC. Over the years, I have seen her occasionally, when our paths cross socially. Our conversations have rarely gone beyond a few words of greeting. As genetics would have it, her voice is the same as our Grandmother Fitz, and it reminds me that this is my first cousin, born only three weeks after me, with whom I shared carefree childhood romps and giggles in our grandmother's yard. I have always regretted not having a closer relationship with my cousins now that our childhood years are well in the past. Maybe too much has transpired: the shared blood may only leave a stain, not a bond. Although my father's brother died in 2020 after a long and happy marriage to his third wife Laurie, I believe his life choices and identity as other than African American have had repercussions that continue to ripple within our family. Sadly, even as they have reached old age, he and my father had not spoken in decades when he died.

As I think back to the trip to Asheville and replay the memories it unearthed, I realize what influence my family history has had in shaping my views. I had always vowed to not allow the painful aspects of our family's heritage and the complicated webs we weave in our search for identity and purpose to cause me to engage in the many sad estrangements that plague members of my family. I will not be complicit, but rather will remain still while those around me stand in their own truth, however they choose to define it. So it is that I respect my brother's embrace of his Native American self. If this will allow him to live in wholeness, to live in peace, rather than to add that to the many challenges he confronts, I am accepting of his choice. If this will allow him to manage the daily struggle with the realities of an America that is clearly not "post-racial," then, again, so be it.

CHAPTER EIGHT

The Hula Dance

As a farewell gesture when I would leave my parents' house and back my car out of the driveway, my mother often did a hula dance followed by curtsies. I loved her signature ritual, as I knew it was a reminder of her forever love and support. When I arrived for an unannounced visit on a Saturday, she greeted me with, "If it isn't La-La. Get in here, girl. Where have you been gallivanting?" Her letters to me were often signed, "Yours until the well runs dry." She also would serenade me when she sensed I was troubled with Diana Ross' "ain't no mountain high enough; ain't no valley low enough; ain't no river wide enough; to keep me from getting to you, babe." She was a graceful dancer, exceptionally light on her feet, and she had a little "bop" move at the core of her freestyle.

When I was a child living in southeast DC, attending public school at Anne Beers Elementary, our family attended St. Timothy's Episcopal Church every Sunday. Before Neal was born, my brother Bruce and I knew we were not to fidget during the service when members of the congregation commented about how much they loved to hear my father read the lessons and passages

Lauri and Mom

from the Bible. Bruce and I waited in anticipation of Mom quietly placing in our hand a lifesaver candy or half a stick of gum. When we moved from 1794 (our southeast DC home) to the new neighborhood, I was scheduled for confirmation in the Episcopal faith (a rite of passage for a teenager) and attended confirmation classes with adults at the church at the top of the hill on my street, Grace Episcopal Church, on Grace Church Road. At Vassar, my first campus job was as a greeter on Sunday mornings at the school chapel.

My mother was an avid reader who shared with me her favorite books and authors as I grew: *The Wind in the Willows*, *Little Women*; poems by Paul Lawrence Dunbar, Robert Frost, and Langston Hughes. Her favorites were Frost's "Stopping by Woods on a Snowy Evening" and Hughes' "Mother to Son," both of which we often recited together. She loved "period" movies; her favorites were *The Prime of Miss Jean Brodie*, *Wuthering Heights*, and *Far from the Madding Crowd*. When I observed my daughter watching *Pride and Prejudice* time after time, treasuring every Harry Potter book and movie, and reading the classics for fun, I knew she had inherited those characteristics from her grandmother. Although my mother was suffering from the debilitating effects of Alzheimer's in later years and was never able to visit her granddaughter in Edinburgh, I knew in my heart that, unlike many others, she would have understood why my daughter Briana has made Edinburgh her home.

My brother Bruce had been born in New York City where we moved to a small basement apartment in my Great Aunt Rita and Great Uncle Clarence's home. Uncle Clarence was a chauffeur at Bergdorf's, and I loved to see his long shiny black car drive up. To my young ears, Aunt Rita talked funny and was from a place called Jamaica. Since we lived in Jamaica, New York, I didn't understand why her daughter Linda, my other cousins, and their friends didn't talk like her.

I always helped Mommy with my baby brother; going to get a clean diaper even before she asked me when I knew it was time for a change and carefully dumping the dirty one into the diaper pail. My neighborhood friend, a boy, and I would press our noses against the aboveground basement window to spy on my mother. One time, he was wide-eyed in awe seeing my mother breastfeed. I stuck close to Mommy much of the time, maybe to keep her in my sight, and to ensure she didn't get away from me again like she had when she had joined Dad in Germany that year.

Mom shared her passion for literature and the English language with her students. They appreciated her rigor and her inspiration, always remembering their seventh-grade English teacher with gratitude and respect. Like her mother, she could be trusted to give an honest and straightforward response when asked, offer solid advice, encouragement, and optimism. She was an accurate judge of character and frightening in her clairvoyance but chose to see the good in everyone. Generous with her financial and emotional support, her sense of humor and fortitude, as the eldest of five children, she became the understated matriarch of the family when my grandmother died. She passed her wisdom to her only surviving youngest sister, Connie, who now fulfills that role so well with her son, Christopher, and with all her nieces, grandnieces, and nephews, dispensing her inherited optimism, good nature, and age-defying boundless energy. She is our beloved "go-to" person for everything.

In Washington, DC, where we moved from New York in 1962, my evening and weekend ballet study required my mother to take me on a succession of public bus rides three days a week. After her long day teaching, we went from one side of the city to the opposite throughout my elementary school years until I was old enough to travel alone. She and I, with my brother Bruce at first, walked to the bus stop, transferring buses once on the way to class. I remember most vividly, however, the frigid dark winter nights when we transferred buses shivering in the cold outside the Harrington Hotel in downtown DC. Mom always prepared dinner when we arrived home after ballet class, and I did my homework, ate, and went to bed. Mom lamented many years later after she bought her beloved red Datsun that she had not gotten her driver's license sooner, because of how much easier life could have been. My brother soon asked to be locked in the house alone rather than take that long journey by bus, which always culminated with him sitting on the indoor steps that led from the house where Miss Jones and Miss Haywood lived, down to the mirrored studio with wooden ballet barres lining the big dance studio's perimeter. He preferred watching the television show *Batman* at home to those long rides and boring hours waiting for his sister.

I cannot thank my mother enough for the ballet classes, and for the long bus rides across town so I could walk into one of the few places a young Black girl could feel completely accepted. I can't thank her enough also for

Lauri and Mayes women. *From left:* Lauri, Great Aunt Alice, Grandma Mayes, Aunt Alice White, cousin Linda White-Ballou, Aunt Connie Scott, Mom, and Aunt LaVerne Davis, *photographer Milton Williams*

teaching me to honor and respect the few unsung Black trailblazers of ballet who forged a quiet trail during extremely difficult times. My mother shared with me the story of Janet Collins, a groundbreaking Black ballerina in the 1950s. Perhaps it is she who inspired my mother's love of ballet. Recently a little slice of Janet Collins' history came to light. She, too, had passed through the doors of Jones-Haywood on her path to unheralded stardom. Sandra showed me a book for children based on Janet Collins' life sent to her by the author, Michelle Meadows. All I can hope is that Janet Collins and so many of the uncelebrated Black ballerinas knew of the few strong and determined women, like my mother, who were inspired by them and who shared their love of ballet with their children.

Family always came first for my mother, so despite allowing Bruce to stay home on those nights when I went to ballet, Bruce and I were always enveloped within our larger extended family. She ensured we grew up near our grandparents, aunts and uncles, and cousins. Neal, who came along much later, missed some of the gatherings that were customary for us.

So it is that whenever I eat a plum, the taste transports me to the warm and safe cocoon of the neighborhood where my mother grew up. "Brentwood" was a small Black enclave near the DC border with Prince George's County, Maryland, officially named North Brentwood to distinguish it from the white section of town. My grandmother's house was the Saturday refuge for our extended family that gathered religiously with food and stories from the week. There was a lot of reminiscing and laughing, accompanied by the sound of the cousins giggling in our all-time hiding place under the dining room table where only the grown folks' shoes could be seen, and their voices heard. So loved was our time together in Brentwood that my cousin Crystal, when she was about seven years old, walked several miles, alone, with her tiny overnight bag from her home in northeast, DC to Grandma's when our Aunt LaVerne, designated to pick her up that afternoon, was slightly delayed.

Whether we were living there temporarily or just visiting, we could count on believing some things would never change. Rituals like shaking almost-ripe plums from the tree in the yard and enjoying the scary antics of my mother's youngest sister, Connie, who was more like the big sister to the rest of the cousins, with only two years separating her in age from her next younger niece. The cousins were more like siblings, and all the nieces slept in the same bed in the doorless "middle bedroom." On many nights, it was wonderful to have so many of us to play endless games of hide-and-seek until the streetlights came on. I also remember running to Grandaddy when he bellowed the name he called me, "La," and I happily ran behind him to the shed, where a huge watermelon rested cooling in the darkness. He would slice it with a large butcher knife, give me the first juicy slice to taste test, and wait until I would nod my head vigorously in the affirmative as the juice ran down my chin.

Great-grandmother
Mayes

Grandaddy Garland
Mayes

When my grandfather was alive, we could always count on a big breakfast with all the Southern charm of hot buttered biscuits, hot cakes, home fries, eggs, sausage, bacon, and rabbit. He was a carpenter, and my grandmother was a domestic in the homes of white people or in the dormitories of white girls at the University of Maryland. My grandparents always managed to have food for everyone on the table and the bills paid from these very humble occupations.

My maternal grandfather Garland Mayes was from Oxford, North Carolina. He shared little about his family and from what we knew, he never ventured back to Oxford. But my grandmother, Marion Herbert Mayes, raised her children and grandchildren in the same neighborhood where she grew up. Over the years, that small house in Brentwood welcomed back home many a child and grandchild, including my mother and me, and later my brother Bruce. It provided a refuge from the trials and tribulations of daily life; if those walls could talk, they would tell stories of pain, laughter, redemption, and wisdom, like those that echoed through so many African American households.

Grandma Marion Mayes

Grandma Mayes had an eighth-grade education but was far more insightful, well read, and progressive than the degreed people I knew. She saw the best in everyone and encouraged everyone, including those relatives hiding "in the closet," to "come out" and be true to who they are. I recall hearing conversations about a male relative who was gay and repeatedly entered relationships with women, many of whom already had children. He ended up raising those children alone when their mothers were either irresponsible or somehow could not support them. Grandma Mayes' acceptance and nonjudgmental attitude about race and sexuality was uncharacteristic of a Black woman of her age. It surfaced unexpectedly in conversations on those legendary Saturdays when we assembled around the dining room table, eating her signature dishes. There were too many dishes that she prepared to single one out as a favorite—everything she cooked was special and laced with her secret ingredients. Everything from collard greens to chocolate cake was made with such love.

In the summers, we often sat on the front porch long into the night, often with one of the girl cousins sitting on a low stool situated between some female relative's open knees as they worked on "combing" our hair. They expertly parted and cornrowed or braided our often thick and tangled locks into submission, dipping the brush into a bowl of water to aid in smoothing the hair, and then worked through with a fingertip's worth of hair pomade from a jar to add shine. Over the years, cornrows were common for the girls in our family as the preferred way to keep our hair neat. We would see more elaborate styles for adults sported by our older female relatives long before they were appropriated and popularized by Bo Derek in the movie 10.

The 4th of July was our favorite holiday, second only to Christmas. Grandma's house was in a prime location to watch the fireworks near the "branch" over the hill beyond the backyard vegetable garden and fence. After an outdoor feast, we awaited sunset when we would pick a comfortable spot to watch the skies light up. I could always count on Aunt 'Verne, my mother's oldest sister, and my Godmother, swatting mosquitoes, which seemed to love her no matter the amount of repellant she sprayed on her body. Linda and Bruce, the cousins who grew up together, having entered the world three weeks apart, played together on those nights. Linda, oldest child of my Aunt Alice, was the first infant subject of my fascination when I accompanied my grandmother to the hospital to bring her and my Aunt Alice back home. I remember my three-year-old big eyes watching my aunt's every move with that baby who looked like one of my dolls come alive.

Sitting or lying out under the stars in the backyard, we children screamed with delight at each sound of the cannon shooting fireworks into the sky, as we anticipated the delay before the sky illuminated in beautiful sparkling-colored patterns or with just flashes of white that looked like lightning. We hated to hear the deafening boom, boom, boom, boom, boom that always preceded the very last fireworks, turning the dark sky into daylight and, as they faded, creating clouds of smoke.

I loved seeing my mother and her only brother Garland, nicknamed Butzie, hand dancing during those long

Mom's siblings. *Back row, from left:* Alice, LaVerne, and Connie; Garland ("Butzie") *in front*

summer nights in Brentwood. Uncle Butzie was always impeccably dressed, and I remember him wiping a speck of dirt off his always vigorously buffed and shiny shoes. His car was equally maintained without a bird dropping, trace of mud, nor cloudy windshield blemishing its perfection.

My mother had a playful side that blossomed when we were with family. Once one of her siblings dared her to go up to the top of the grassy levy bordering the branch and dance, in a spot that could be viewed from the backyard by us, and by any neighbors on that strip. Of course, she complied, to our applause and shouts of delight.

As Brentwood was the neighborhood where my mother grew up, three of her sisters and a brother lived a half block from Grandma and Grandaddy in adjacent houses—Great Aunt Kate, Great Aunt Mabel, and Great Uncle Charlie in one house, and Great Aunt Alice next door. Hard workers all, Aunt Kate and Aunt Mabel were the best-dressed women I had ever seen, and I thought they both were elegant and fashionable. Aunt Kate loved the color lavender and wore it well. When I think of her, it is always in a lavender dress, with a powdered face and a bit of rouge on her cheeks.

Great Aunt Mabel and
Grandma Mayes

Great-grandma Herbert

They lived in a corner house with a big yard, bedecked with roses and peonies, and with a vegetable garden in the back. While the sisters at that end of the street rarely visited each other, they always waved to each other from their respective yards and greeted each other lovingly with the words, "skee week." This also was the greeting the Alpha Kappa Alpha sorority trademarked. I am not sure of its origin and have no idea what possibly could have connected the Herbert family and the AKAs. Another novel phrase used by my grandmother was, "Aw betch," which she would say to us children whenever she dried our tears and comforted us when we scraped a knee or were unhappy for any reason.

I loved to visit that house with the big wide swing on the porch where we would sit with the Great Aunts and sometimes Great Uncle Charlie, rocking back and forth maybe too vigorously until we were gently told to slow down, while we sucked on "penny candy" from Mr. Wallace's store or, if we were really lucky, a popsicle from the "ice cream man's" truck, which arrived blasting its trademark jingle every summer evening. I remember particularly liking the popsicles that turned my lips blue or the white ones that tasted like lemonade.

My grandmother's house also exposed me to the many ways in which African American families are a blend of African, European, and Native American heritage. Our family was replete with adults and children of many hues of brown. Sisters and brothers with the same birth parents varied widely in their features and skin tone, and some treated differently based on skin color. Colorism is ugly, but it is also unfortunately quite pervasive across African American families. In ways great and small, it was clear to me that the system in place in our country made it easier for the "light, bright, and damned near white," to succeed. But as much as we weaponize color in our communities, Africans, just like their brothers and sisters on this side of the Atlantic, also come in all colors of the spectrum. I have an example close to my heart that helps me reflect on this. My son Fernando was born of two brown-skinned, brown-eyed Angolan parents, and he inherited light skin and light eyes. Despite that, it is still tough to see the impact of colorism up close in my own family. When my daughter Briana was young, for example, she asked her grandmother if she was white, a question that was met with a chuckle and a definitive "no" from my mother. That Briana has become such an advocate for people of color, for women, and for the environment, is a testament to the work of our family, her parents, and especially the work she has done to move past the narrow limitations placed on us by a racially divided society. The progeny of the Mayes, Herbert, Hawkins, Fitts, and Fitz families have lived with the same negative messages about blackness that all African American families have had to endure, and as I look at our dwindling family group today, I am proud that we have survived, thrived, and overcome, and that we live our lives in peace and grace.

My elementary school years were peppered with pivotal events. In 1963, when I was in the third grade in South-east Washington, DC, Bruce and I waited, like we did every day, on the front steps of our house after walking home from school. Mommy soon arrived from teaching, and I could see that she was frightened and had been crying. She hurriedly unlocked the front door, went straight to the television, and I heard Walter Cronkite say, "President John F. Kennedy was shot minutes ago." We sat with her quietly that day and the following days watching the re-plays of Jack Ruby being shot, and of the funeral proces-sion, as we wondered what else could possibly happen.

I wrote the name "Martin Luther King, Jr." on a small scrap of paper that I hid in a centrally and quickly ac-cessible drawer of the buffet in the dining room of our house in southeast DC. I memorized it because my fa-ther told me to never forget that name. A few years lat-er, when I knew the name well, and not just his name but who the man was, Dr. King was assassinated. I saw the sadness and sense of loss reflected on the faces of all in the circle that defined my world. I was shocked and confused when Dad drove the family to see the still smoldering and vandalized buildings and destruction of downtown DC, which was real, not like what I saw on television during those dark and frightening days. Through the windows of our car, we could see what happens when masses of Black people are angry, griev-ing, and aggrieved. I saw the muddy "Resurrection City" campsite created in protest by colored people from near and far demanding civil rights, justice, and recognition of the racism ravaging our country two hundred years after our enslaved ancestors were "freed." The campsite was located on the hallowed grounds of the Washington Mall with occupants staining the view of monuments erected to honor a country whose citizens were not all accorded equal status.

Just a few months later, in June 1968, Bobby Kennedy was assassinated during the presidential campaign when he hoped to follow in his brother's footsteps and become president of the US. The lyrics of the haunting song "Abraham, Martin, and John," still reverberate. "Has anybody here seen my old friend Bobby, Can you tell me where he's gone? I thought I saw him walkin' up over the hill with Abraham, Martin, and John."

In 1967, we moved from our Black neighborhood in southeast DC to an all-white neighborhood in Silver Spring, Maryland. I had grown accustomed to a predominantly Black elementary school and living in an all-Black neighborhood where I played kickball and jacks with children who looked like me, on the cement steps outside our houses, until we wore holes in the seats of our pants. In so many ways, it was a huge adjustment to move to Silver Spring.

I ached for the comfort of my all-Black southeast DC neighborhood. I had moved from the security of a neighborhood wedged between Southern Avenue and Alabama Avenue, on the border of DC and Maryland's Prince George's County. It was "on the other side of the river," a designation assigned by those more affluent, mostly white people on the opposite shore of the Anacostia River. These dividing lines were most often railroad tracks like the one I had to traverse via a rickety wooden bridge at the top of the hill on my new street. It divided the white neighborhood where I now lived from the blacker enclave on the other side. Because I lived on the white side of the tracks and was the new kid, the Black kids who led the powerful cliques on the other side did not readily welcome me. I didn't quite fit in, although I did learn a lot from the most militant of the group who "walked the walk and talked the talk" of the popular Black Panthers. His nickname was Po'k Chop, and his sister Robyn and I became friendly in high school; she and I still have fun when we run into each other in and around DC.

I only learned later that there was a reason why rail-road tracks separated our majority white neighborhood from the neighborhood where people of color lived. The separation was deliberate. This practice, called "redlining," was historically employed to perpetuate segregation. Baltimore was its first target in 1937, but it would not be long before neighborhoods across the country came to reflect this ugly agenda. Cartographers in Baltimore drafted a "redlining map that used the colors red, yellow, blue, and green to identify neighborhoods based on potential risk factors for residential mortgage holders. Areas marked in red and called "Fourth Grade" or "D" were characterized by "detrimental influence in a pronounced degree. Undesirable population, low percentage of home ownership, poor maintenance and a prevalence of vandalism." As distasteful as it may be to think about, the practice of "redlining" began with the National Housing Act of 1934, which established the Federal Housing Administration. The assumptions in redlining resulted in a large increase in residential racial segregation. Redlining meant that my life in Silver Spring was divided along color lines in a way that I had never experienced in earlier days in southeast DC. While I had spent my entire life to that point with children of color who accepted me implicitly, my family's new life in a house on the white side of the bridge separated me from my natural community and exposed me to a world I had not previously known, but one I would come to learn to traverse. Maneuvering on both sides of the bridge meant that I learned early to code switch, to talk in the lexicon and tone required for the audience and circumstance, and to be comfortable performing on any stage.

When we moved to Silver Spring, Maryland, it was hardly more than a decade since the landmark *Brown v. Board of Education* decision in 1954 in which the US Supreme Court determined that state laws establishing racial segregation in public schools were unconstitutional.

To me, the desegregation of public schools felt like an adagio that wasn't well choreographed and was definitely not lyrical. This was much the way I viewed my acceptance among my schoolmates within the majority culture. I was required to compete academically and socially in this majority white environment, as I became a living experiment in school integration. And despite stellar grades throughout high school, I will never forget that when I wanted to take an Advanced Placement (AP) English class, a teacher informed me that my IQ was not high enough. I didn't recall ever taking an IQ test, and knew with certainty that her desire to bar me from the class had nothing to do with whether my IQ was high or not. Instead, what I had come to understand is that I lacked a de-melanated complexion. I may not have had the highest IQ, but I certainly had the emotional intelligence to know that I was being excluded because of my race.

A few dozen Black students and I integrated Montgomery (Montgy/ "Monkey") Hills Junior High School. I was the only Black person in most of my classes from seventh through ninth grades. Add to that: pressure, puberty, moving to a new neighborhood, and everything else that comes with being a tween suddenly swimming in the deep end of the pool. So it was that during that awkward, transitional year for all of us—seventh grade— I found solace in my friendship with Bob Kroll. He came to my rescue with a joke, a smile, a wave . . . and help with math. In return, I briefed him on books he never read so that he could present his required book reports. With my assistance and with his unfailing charm, which he turned on for fellow students as well as teachers, Bob's presentations of his book reports were flawless! His delivery was so convincing that even I was astounded as I sat and listened in class with just the tiniest smirk on my face.

I had one particularly loyal Black friend, Tiawana, who lived on the other side of the bridge. I remember crossing

Bob Kroll, *courtesy of Bob Kroll*

the rickety, one-car only, wooden bridge over the railroad tracks to attend her brother's wedding in their backyard. His name was Tor, and we called him El Toro (the bull in Spanish). He wed a young white woman whose family did not attend the event as they did not approve of the marriage. The couple was incredibly young and soon discovered the hardships that accompanied young interracial love in those days.

Another two African American girls became my friends during those teenage years. In junior high I was joined by Keyna Foster, the daughter of one of my mother's childhood friends from Brentwood. She became a popular cheerleader and dated a star basketball player who she eventually married. Another surprise friend, Mitzi Young, who attended Anne Beers Elementary School with me, reentered my life in high school at Bethesda-Chevy Chase (B-CC). She and my best friend in elementary school, Alethea Smith, remain in my circle of friends today.

My family had just moved to the new neighborhood in 1967, and Mom was pregnant with my younger brother Neal. Soon after his birth, when she entered an extended period of postpartum depression, my guide to comfort and some acceptance at school was Bob. Why we bonded may have been connected to his family. Resembling the white side of his family, he did not fit the stereotypical image of a half-Latino youth, with his platinum blonde hair and blue eyes. He was somewhat conversant in Spanish, having been raised by his Puerto Rican mother and maternal grandmother (who was very much a woman of color). He and I shared a level of comfort that others might not have completely understood. We became confidantes early when he shared with me that his parents were divorcing. His mother and I connected immediately, and I began babysitting for his three younger siblings. By the time the three of them reached the seventh grade, his family had moved to another school district. Interestingly, they attended Eastern Junior High School, where each one in turn was in my mother's English class. I always felt at home and embraced by Bob's large Catholic family of five children.

Since then, Bob and I have been close friends; that's over fifty years of crises of the heart and home, through marriages and divorces. Our connection has always been uncanny no matter the distance or time between our reunions. We even discovered, under surprising circumstances, that Bob had randomly selected my cousin when he became a "Big Brother" to a young boy in Arizona where he has lived most of his adult life. Unbeknownst to me, the boy's mother and his siblings, who are my New York cousins, had decided to move to Phoenix. They soon became Bob's surrogate family. This is the family of one of the sons of my Jamaican Aunt Rita, in whose basement apartment we had lived all those many years ago. Bob's commitment to this now adult man and his family, ironically, may partially explain what ties him inextricably to life in the Arizona desert, even after retirement from an incredible government career in Native American affairs. While most of his family, roots, and loving friends are miles away in his native DC, Bob lives quite contentedly in an oasis in the desert. In recent years, I've found that I miss my friend more as we age and recognize how much shared history, familiarity, comfort, and emotional attachment can sustain relationships beyond time and distance.

I did form a few other school friendships over time with girls and boys who invited me to their parties and coming-of-age events. Most of our classmates were Jewish, and I was invited to bar and bat mitzvahs. I knew, even then, that these invitations were gestures of genuine inclusion. But my interactions with these classmates were not without some discomfort. I remember one particularly difficult encounter on a quiet morning after the bus dropped me off at school. I usually studied with a group of my white classmates in the mornings before school began. At some point, I had changed my hairstyle and wore my hair in a natural, and what I thought was a quite becoming style. Well, teenagers can be quite direct, and offhand comments are their norm, so one of the boys asked if I had been shocked by an electrical current. Although the comment generated peals of laughter, and I joined in, I hoped my laughter would cover my deep embarrassment and hurt feelings.

When I then went to high school, I crossed that wooden bridge over the tracks daily to catch the bus with other Black kids bussed to Bethesda-Chevy Chase High School. I can't count how many times I have watched the Denzel Washington movie, *Remember the Titans*, because it is based on a true story, which takes place at T. C. Williams High School in nearby Alexandria, Virginia, during the same time frame that I was in high school and reminds me so much of those years.

It was also while I was at B-CC that I met the young man who checked all the boxes and more in my heart. My first serious boyfriend, Ailue attended the revered all-male HBCU Morehouse College, in Atlanta, and alma mater of Martin Luther King, Jr. When we started dating, I was still at the same high school he had attended three years ahead of me, so we had never met in high school. He came from a family of six children, and I knew one of his younger brothers, a star basketball player at our high school. I became friends with the basketball player's older sister Litra, and soon met their handsome, older brother, and Morehouse man. Ailue and I were straight out of "central casting". We shared many things in common—physical attraction, compatibility, family and culture, and an ability to adapt and fit into any environment. I was nervous when I asked my father for permission to go with him and his friend to see a movie, *Fiddler on the Roof*. It was our first date. Long before texting, we wrote sweet love letters to each other, and I counted the days and hours until he returned home for holidays and summers. I couldn't contain my joy every time we were reunited after weeks or months apart. I loved the summer evenings when we would drive to Hains Point at the southern tip of East Potomac Park between the Potomac River and the Washington Channel, and we would walk to the banks of the river and lean against the railing feeling the breeze gently brush the day's humidity away. He was pursued by the Spelman College crowd, Morehouse's sister school, and although we hung onto the relationship by a string for several rocky years, I was young and insecure, and surrendered our storybook romance to the distance between Atlanta and Poughkeepsie, New York, where Vassar is located.

After teaching English for many years, Mom retired, but she soon returned to substitute teach at an elementary school "over the bridge," Rosemary Hills Elementary School. My mother crossed that divide in her later years to teach kindergarten children, a grade level she said she never wanted to teach but had come to love in her postretirement years. There have been many days when

I thanked God that my daughter grew up with that ideal grandmother who spoiled her, shared family traditions, and loved her deeply as only a grandmother can.

Now that I am a parent and grandparent, I have learned that the key is to get to know your children well and to anticipate how best to help them define their own path, to provide them the best opportunities, and to facilitate access to essential skill sets. Try as I might, my youngest occasionally reminds me where I have fallen short, and I feel I surpassed expectations with my two older children. When she was eleven years old, Briana experienced the turmoil of adjusting to a small city apartment in a new neighborhood after moving from the only home she had known in the spacious suburbs. She also had to adjust to living with me, the parent who had not been as available to her as her father.

I now realize that I was about the same age when my youngest brother, Neal, was born months after we moved to the new house on Grace Church Road in Silver Spring. It was a decidedly difficult year as I faced so much change, including my budding adolescence, and the "absence" of the mother I knew; it was perhaps the worst year of my childhood. Mom suffered from a deep postpartum depression for almost a year after Neal was born, virtually paralyzing her and leaving her unable to function. I was fully aware of how painful that year was for her, for me, and for our family. It didn't help that I was in the throes of puberty, was an impressionable and needy twelve-year-old, had entered a new school, and was living in a new neighborhood.

How ironic that history repeated itself; I entered a deep depression when Briana was adjusting to similar life changes. I did confide in my parents, as well as a few relatives and good friends who were there through that period and who have been consistent in their support and love. My first bout with depression occurred when my husband and I were still together. The second was after we finally separated, and Briana and I moved to a small apartment in the Dupont Circle area of DC.

I value to this day the friendship and support I received from Liz Joslin and from Hege Wade, the mothers of the two girls in the rock band with my daughter Briana. As I made the leap to being a single mother, it became quite evident that it was "more than a notion" to raise a child alone. All I could do was keep it together enough to work and care for Briana. I have come to learn that mood disorders are on both sides of my family, although they are more prevalent in my paternal relatives. I remember my husband telling me that Black people don't suffer from depression or turn to the services of therapists. That view is common among many Africans and African Americans, and, thankfully, is starting to be debunked. Having been through this myself and been there for family and friends in their time of need, I know that effective treatment is essential and can help people to lead productive lives free from pain, stigma, and ridicule.

I talked with my mother a lot during these periods as she knew firsthand what I was experiencing. I worked so hard to appear "normal" and supportive, and to uphold my responsibilities as a newly single mother. During that period, it was difficult to take Briana to soccer practices and games, attend parent meetings at school, and go to her football games, all while focusing on my work. I moved twice that year and faced the biggest challenge of my life at that time, to stay on track, and to survive. We, African American women, are expected to be strong in every circumstance; we do not allow ourselves the luxury of failure.

From my early years, I not only easily learned the Spanish language but also felt a deep, inexplicable connection and comfort among the people for whom Spanish is their native tongue. Perhaps this started with the

Brothers Neal and Bruce

periods of time that I lived in Spain, the Dominican Republic, and Mexico. The familiarity, involvement, and sense of community is genuine and has become a defining dimension at T. C. Williams High School in nearby Alexandria, Virginia, which I know is uncharacteristic of many African American women of my generation. Again, I reflect on how unusual it was for my mother, a Black woman in the United States in the 1960s, to encourage her young daughter to learn a foreign language; it has been a gift for which I cannot thank her enough.

In her mid-'70s, my mother was diagnosed with Alzheimer's disease. Dad and Bruce, who had a complicated and difficult history with each other, managed to live together as her caregivers for several years until her death. While Neal and I mourn the loss of our mother, the sibling most devastated is her middle child, Bruce, who needed and benefited most from her never-ending support, no matter where he was in his often-painful cycle of life.

When our father asked him to return home, Bruce immediately agreed and shared responsibility for our mother's last several years. Both our father and Bruce suffered the stress of all long-term caretakers' fatigue. My dad's attitude toward me reinforced my feelings of guilt and regret that my time with her over her last years was largely limited to weekend visits, given my frequent professional travel schedule and all my other responsibilities. I treasure the time I did spend with her on Saturdays before the disease ravaged her brain. She always expressed a combination of embarrassment and gratitude when I would help her into a warm, fragrant bathtub (before she grew frightened of the water), gently bathed her, and applied her favorite lemon or lavender potions on her baby-soft skin. She was always so humble, unassuming, and found it difficult to accept kindness, but was generous to a fault with her thank-yous.

Mom confided in me and I in her. She was wise and, like her mother, shared so many nuggets of wisdom that have guided me. Her youngest sister, Connie, and I have always been close, and we often recall her guidance that touched our lives and those of so many family members, friends, and her students. As the fates would have it, my mother left this earth on the eve of Briana's graduation from the University of Edinburgh.

Anticipating her passing before I left for Scotland, I arranged for St. Alban's Associate Rector, Jim Quigley, to join us at her bedside in the living room at home where we had moved her those last weeks, for her final holy communion. I knew in my soul that she would soon transition, and I would not see her again. Dad, Bruce, Neal, Connie, and I, were led in prayer by Jim over her withering body and barely accessible mind. She opened her eyes in what appeared a fleeting moment of recognition. I found my peace at that moment and was able to contain my grief for 24 hours after Dad called to tell me she was gone. Briana's father, her brother, and I were in Edinburgh attending an evening pre-graduation celebration with her friends' families. I did not want to ruin her big day, so I waited to tell them about Mom's passing until our family dinner at the end of all the pomp and circumstance of her graduation day.

Joyce Mayes Fitz's relationship with each of us was uniquely abundant and cherished. But it was I who received the blessing of that special ritual that she had always reserved just for me: the hula dance and curtsy in the driveway of the home, where she lived and died, on Grace Church Road.

CHAPTER NINE

The Tap Dance

I studied and performed classical ballet, modern dance, and jazz, but had few formal tap classes. Nonetheless, Miss Jones, the founder with Claire Haywood of Jones-Haywood School of Ballet, was an accomplished tap dancer and teacher and included several tap pieces in our Capitol Ballet repertoire. Like Doris Jones, several of our company members had studied tap and were also accomplished dancers in that genre. Dancing side by side with them on stage could be daunting if I allowed myself to go to that place of self-doubt. So, I drew upon what was familiar and came to me naturally—musicality: the rhythm of the steps; technique; and proper upper body placement. Core control allowed the legs and feet freedom of movement; precision of the steps; and feeling grounded in the movements rather than elevated as is intended in ballet. Tap required me to draw upon the technique I had learned in my study of other dance genres to quickly learn the mechanics of the unfamiliar movements by practicing the choreography with the help of my colleagues and, at show time, matching my colleagues' skill with my fearlessness, projecting confidence, and radiating the joy in the sounds of the synchronized clicks of our taps.

In recent years, my friend and former US ambassador Sally Shelton-Colby and I have taken a few tap classes taught by our friend, Kay Casstevens. I have followed in Kay's footsteps, as she, too, has had a long career in government, policy, and politics, followed by a return to arts-related passions in her second chapter at the National Gallery of Art teaching tap and choreographing for local theater groups. I believe she feels about tap the way I feel about ballet. I am sure we share the same rush when the sound of everyone's clicking tap shoes resonate in unison. My many years in public affairs and lobbying often felt like a tap dance as I was constantly striving for that unified resonance, although sometimes the outcome was an unwanted and undesirable dissonance.

In the eyes of various US executive administrations, members of Congress, the media, and the public, being a lobbyist means wearing a "scarlet letter" of sorts. It is an industry that has withstood a level of scrutiny stirred up over the last decade by some bad actors and trends that are associated with corruption and negative political influence. Lobbying is a very misunderstood profession.

Even now, as I look back on my career from the safety of a healthy and happy new chapter, I am conflicted about the last fifteen years of my career as a lobbyist at The Livingston Group (TLG). To be fair, early in my professional trajectory after leaving the Foreign Service, the eleven years I spent representing countries, companies, organizations, and personalities at Gray and Company and Hill and Knowlton, were not without conflict, controversy, and challenging clients. Young, but having lived and worked in three foreign countries before I turned thirty, I transitioned from diplomacy to the private sector in public affairs and strategic communications at Gray and Company quickly, only three weeks after resigning from the Foreign Service. I learned the ropes and assumed major responsibility representing Robert Maxwell, the larger-than-life British media mogul; singer John Denver; Werner Erhard, the creator of transformational learning/EST training; Citizens for a Free Kuwait (a group formed after Saddam Hussein's Iraqi forces, in violation of international law, invaded and occupied their country); the Government of Haiti; a liberation party in Angola; and advising clients about the evolution of the antiapartheid movement and implications of sanctions against South Africa.

In the early 1980s, Gray and Company was the new kid on the block, and it soon became the boutique trendsetter and the standard bearer for public affairs. We had the coolest open offices in an old powerhouse located on the C&O Canal in high-end Georgetown. Our address had no street number, and not even a street name: it was simply The Powerhouse, Washington, DC. We made the most of our cutting-edge status with state-of-the-art technology displayed in a glass-enclosed room with major network news broadcast on various wall-mounted screens and a teletype machine noisily printing breaking stories on long continuous scrolls of paper monitored by eager interns who tore off important items and distributed them to the relevant client teams and division leaders. It was a friendly, fun, exciting, vibrant, bipartisan atmosphere of multidisciplinary services. Staff included lobbyists led by Gary Hymel, former speaker of the house Tip O'Neill's staffer from Louisiana, and public relations experts led by Frank Mankiewicz (son of Herman Mankiewicz, the Oscar-winning screenwriter of *Citizen Kane*), who had been Regional Director for Latin America at the Peace Corps, head of National Public Radio, and, as press secretary, the person remembered for having announced sadly to the world that yet another Kennedy, Bobby, had been assassinated. And, as though it wasn't enough that the international division was already steeped in intrigue, my international staff colleagues and I reached our desks by climbing a spiral staircase to an open crow's nest, high above the rest of the offices, where we had a bird's-eye view of all the activity below.

My years at Gray and Company, twenty years before my time at The Livingston Group, perhaps were inevitably different from those at TLG; they had such different cultures despite sharing similar professions. My work at Gray focused on developing and implementing holistic, multidisciplinary approaches to problem solving and promotion of client policy interests, including securing print and broadcast media coverage and developing other communication vehicles; developing core media messages; and providing rigorous media training, promotion and, education of clients and relevant audiences. At TLG, I applied the same skills, honed earlier in my career, for a panoply of clients, though it was clear to all that the primary and familiar method to achieve client goals was through our core business—lobbying. We advocated primarily with legislators—senators and representatives, and their staff on Capitol Hill. In fact, Bob Livingston, a former congressman from Louisiana, had created the firm with former staff upon leaving Capitol Hill in 1999.

My service in government or the private sector had not been primarily engagement with the Hill; specifically, before TLG, I had served in government during five administrations—Nixon, Ford, Carter, Reagan and Clinton, and my public and private sector work had been rooted in diplomacy, both cultural and commercial. In the private sector, in addition to Gray and Company and Hill and Knowlton, I was a senior executive at a telecommunications/satellite start-up, supporting teams through a public offering, a product launch, and a Chapter 11 filing. I also had served on multiple nonprofit boards.

Much like those in the military, I understood that effective diplomats are supposed to leave partisan views at home. This was how I started as a professional even though I dove into the deep end of the political pool quickly thereafter, starting with my various roles working with Ron Brown. Many of my lasting relationships with members of Congress and staff, and my techniques in advocacy and negotiating, were developed while observing him. I also knew many members through my work with congressional districts throughout the US. In my role in the Commerce Department. I opened commercial offices and managed not only a branch of the Foreign Service at Commerce and its vast domestic operation of 90 offices, all strategically located in cities across the country supporting the marketing and export of products for constituents important to state and local officials, and to members of Congress. Exports were of burgeoning importance to the US economy, generating not only employment but higher-paying jobs. Indeed, the Department of Commerce coordinated the development of the first "National Export Strategy" for the nation.

My accumulated experience and strengths were in developing strategies and employing a multidisciplinary approach to engage policy makers and influencers in the federal government, the private sector, inside think tanks, among special interest groups, and with activists. The teams at TLG, on the other hand, placed more importance on the congressional landscape where most of our colleagues and consultants either had been members of Congress or their staffers. This became abundantly clear to me when I heard, directly or indirectly, comments like "The Commerce Department is not an important federal agency," or "She couldn't find her way around the Hill if her life depended on it."

Clearly, my skill set and approach were radically different from those of my colleagues; my array of professional, political, and life experiences often elicited from them consternation or discomfort about my "take" on client issues and solutions. Therefore, at TLG, the differences that separated me from my colleagues were magnified; they were appreciated by some, barely tolerated by others, and even, on occasion, disparaged by a few. When we worked as a team, embracing our complementary skill, the client goals inevitably were more efficiently and successfully achieved—our tap shoes clicked with unified precision. Much too often, however, I reverted to that unrelenting "hamster wheel" for people who, like me, hail from a marginalized and underrepresented community—I understood I had to prove myself by working harder and smarter. I also came to recognize the strategic importance of biting my tongue more often than not, despite my credentials, track record, breadth of experience, deep knowledge of the art of diplomacy, and trade and communication skills. I longed for the familiar and comfortable professional respect and social atmosphere I had enjoyed at Gray and Company/H&K (acquired by Hill and Knowlton in 1986), no matter our politics. Instead of being truly bipartisan, TLG was undeniably a partisan space, and I was in the minority in every sense of the word, particularly after Democrats Toby Moffett (who introduced me to Bob Livingston and with whom I joined The Livingston Group), a former member of Congress from Connecticut, Dennis Hertel, a former member of Congress from Michigan, and Stacie Walters Fujii, an insightful African American former Hill staffer with a vast network on Capitol Hill and strategic plan acumen, all left the firm. They were my colleagues as well as my friends and our camaraderie extended to after hours, rarely the case with my other senior peers. I did develop valued relationships with some of my colleagues at TLG, and I was extremely touched when many of them attended the service when my mother passed.

I also had many exceptional interns at TLG. One of my partners, Bernie Robinson, a self-described independent, hosts fund-raisers in his comfortable and convenient Capitol Hill home for elected officials and candidates of both political parties. I was a frequent guest at these events. He was always welcoming and available for conversations over breakfast. In addition, I valued the shared experience of working with Steve Bende and the team on representing the Cleveland Clinic. Several personal relationships with colleagues continued after my tenure at TLG including Marjery Strayer, Dave Loney, and Dick Rogers.

To be candid, in the early stages of my career at Gray and Company, regardless of whether clients and their goals were in or outside of my comfort zone, I usually felt confident that my colleagues had my back. As a partner at TLG, expected to generate revenue and lead the international practice, I took my work obligations seriously, and much like a lawyer, represented clients with politics and practices contrary to my own. At this stage of my career, I had fully developed political views, and increasingly found myself in personal turmoil over the compromises expected of me to fulfill my obligations to colleagues and clients, while meeting my own high-performance standards. These were in no small way instilled in me through my years of discipline in the practice of dance, and by my parents. There were many occasions when representing a controversial client was truly a "heavy lift," as my TLG partner Allen Martin often said. He and I worked together most often, and, although our politics were at opposite ends of the spectrum, we respected each other and had the ability to find humor in untenable client demands and laughed at the stories we exchanged about our respective amusing personal family dynamics.

In general, stepping away or recusing myself from a task or client was an impractical professional option.

Truth be told, I learned along the way that internalizing battles of conscience results in self-inflicted scars and keloids, leading to sometimes crippling stress. Perhaps, as a coping mechanism, I learned to translate my lobbying work into a process—educate the parties involved, reposition the requested outcomes to what was feasible, and draw upon my diplomatic, public affairs, communications, and corporate experience to inform my path.

Over the years, I have learned that the American body politic is all too often insular and/or entitled and guilty of conscious and unconscious bias. Many engaged in policymaking are limited in their grasp of issues and don't want to do the homework to truly understand the roots of conflicts, and the problems confronting our bilateral relationships with the unknown and the unfamiliar. Seeking to understand others' different perspectives and unfamiliar lifestyles, and practices is critical to developing *cultural competence*, an essential and missing element in resolving all issues influenced by disparities and differences—historical, political, socioeconomic— within our country and with other countries. I've also found that we rarely respect those who are professionally tasked with helping us gain the knowledge about a "truth" other than our own. Finally, our complex process of regulatory, legislative, and policy formulation is most often a conundrum for those who did not grow up in the United States, and sometimes even for those who did.

It was rewarding to work on many issues that had a genuine positive impact and that saved and transformed lives. If an issue would lead to political stability, grow an economy, increase the respect for human rights, and provide an opportunity for social and policy change, then I was all in. I have worked on lifting sanctions, normalizing diplomatic relations, advocating for trade agreements, and negotiating resolutions to political crises. Although I was able to feel a sense of accomplishment from my interactions with clients, in some cases my clients were unpredictable, negative lightning rods, no matter how I tried to realistically set expectations and parse their stated and unstated objectives and agendas.

Bar none, my experience working on the Kuwait account while at H&K was controversial and challenging from day one. For more than a decade, the Kuwait account and my involvement have engendered negative and vicious criticism, private and public stress, and pain. Despite what I had learned, practiced, and endured during the rigors of my dance training, I was unprepared for this experience. It left me feeling like collateral damage.

It all started before the 1990 Gulf War when Iraq invaded Kuwait, and it remains a topic of debate even in campaigns today. If you lived it, you know that the Gulf War was a political quagmire, and that there has been a great deal of analysis that attempts to explain how public opinion about the war was shaped.

I was a senior vice president and international practice director at Hill and Knowlton. The client, vetted by H&K, was a group of Kuwaiti exiles, who, after their country was invaded, organized a group called Citizens for a Free Kuwait (CFK). These apparently wealthy, concerned Kuwaiti exiles, lived predominantly in the US and Britain, having escaped an Iraqi invasion that separated their families and disrupted their lives. They were experiencing the results of lasting physical and mental trauma. The Iraqi occupation of Kuwait was a clear violation of international law declared so by the US Government. H&K was hired by CFK to educate and inform the US public about Kuwait, a remote country far away from America's public consciousness, and about the facts and repercussions facing the Kuwaiti people in the wake of the invasion. My understanding was that H&K's mandate was not about encouraging or supporting US military action against Iraq, nor were any H&K programs designed for that purpose.

At the time, Citizens for a Free Kuwait was the public relations industry's single largest account, paying H&K $13 million over six months for its services. As we knew it would be, the media attention was unrelenting. After all, CFK was a foreign entity, controversial, and concerned with building understanding for a group of people little known and indeed looked at with suspicion in America—Arabs, and Muslims. Shamefully, even today, almost thirty years later, too many Americans still hold on to negative stereotypes about this part of the world.

I was the account manager and the main public spokesperson for H&K. In this role, I was the subject of incessant scrutiny, inaccurate reporting, and politically slanted accounts of events, in both print and broadcast media, and later, in books.

Specifically, H&K coordinated a hearing with the House of Representatives' Human Rights Caucus, co-chaired by Democratic congressman Tom Lantos and Republican congressman John Porter. This broadly covered hearing was the genesis of what later became my long nightmare. My credentials, credibility, morals, and professionalism were challenged and undermined; everything I had worked so hard to establish was under threat, and all because of an inaccurate, partisan controversy, and some genuine misunderstandings.

The primary controversy arose from the anonymous testimony of a young witness who described personally observing babies being removed by Iraqi soldiers from incubators in a Kuwaiti hospital. The resulting controversy boiled down to whether this actually occurred, whether the witness was telling the truth, and the identity of the anonymous witness. Exacerbating the controversy, the testimony was repeated by President George H.W. Bush in speeches that were then used by politicians to build support for US military action against Iraq. I was caught in the crosshairs of a combination of biased accounts of events and political cross fire between both supporters and opponents of subsequent US military action against Iraq.

At that hearing, the teenage girl who made the statement was identified by CFK and was one of several potential witnesses. H&K had been told that she was in Kuwait with family members when she had witnessed Iraqi soldiers taking babies out of incubators in a hospital. We had evidence that she was in Kuwait at the time, and her story was consistent with other reports of abuses recorded by human rights organizations. It was agreed that she and other witnesses at the hearing would not be named; they would remain anonymous, both for their own protection, and to protect their family members still in Kuwait and under Iraqi occupation. The young witness at the hearing was the daughter of the Kuwaiti Ambassador to the US.

When the press discovered and revealed her identity, their accounts impugned her credibility. Perhaps naively, my team members and I did not perceive her familial connections as a reason to doubt the truthfulness of her memory of the events she recounted. Further, her eyewitness account was consistent with other independent reports by reputable human rights organizations. Our pledge to keep her identity secret, with the approval of the hearing, only added suspicion that this was staged by H&K to incite a US policy response.

The required H&K registration, a matter of public record, disclosed the unprecedented fee Hill and Knowlton had received, which placed it at the center of attention of the producers at 60 Minutes. They reached out to H&K to set up an interview for a segment on 60 Minutes. I was encouraged to take the interview and to speak about the account and the hearing. No one from among the senior H&K management expressed any concerns about me doing the interview. Craig Fuller was George H.W. Bush's chief of staff when he was vice president. In 1990, Bush was president and Fuller was chief operating officer of Hill and Knowlton. Parenthetically, I was several months pregnant at the time.

In her infinite wisdom, my friend and colleague Jill Schuker had advised me *not* to appear for the *60 Minutes* interview, saying that the approach to be taken by the show likely would not be sympathetic. But I was resolute in my conviction that the firm's actions with respect to this client were appropriate. I also was confident that I was up to the task and that, as the account supervisor, it was my responsibility to explain to the world H&K's honorable intent and actions. Little did I know that my superiors, capitalizing on my unfettered zeal to defend the firm, were relieved that I was willing to be the one to go on the air—the public face. The outcome was that I felt I had been thrown under the bus.

Well, I certainly had my 15 minutes of "fame", and I have been haunted by those 15 minutes for two decades. First came the highly critical and incendiary editorials in the *Wall Street Journal*, the *New York Times*, and *Harper's Magazine*, attacking me personally. And later, when it mattered most—during the Senate confirmation hearings for my Commerce Department appointment—all this negative press coverage and this interview were powerful tools against me, creating doubt about my credibility.

Further complicating matters, there were press reports that the CFK funding came from the Government of Kuwait, further undermining Nayirah's story (her name was revealed by the press) and alleging that I was complicit in all of it. In the course of time, and after H&K's representation ended, it came to light that much of the CFK funding was indeed from the Government of Kuwait, a fact that was not known to me during our representation.

I am forever grateful to Morton Kondracke, a respected moderate conservative opinion writer, and Eric Holder, then the US attorney for DC and later US Attorney General in the Obama administration, who both provided their support in written editorials that came armed with the facts. Eric and I had known each other since he was at Columbia Law School, and he was able to address both the facts of the matter as well as me personally, thereby providing a vital and incisive validation.

The rending of my reputation lasted for years and haunted me relentlessly. I firmly believe that if I were a white male, these events would not have unfolded in such a vitriolic way. I have believed that my actions as account supervisor were ethical and honest. I am also confident that I performed credibly, with integrity, and to the best of my ability with the information I had at the time. I stand by my every perception of the facts and my actions.

Two years after the events, this issue loomed large and became a factor for Democratic and Republican senators who initially blocked my confirmation to the Commerce Department. The confirmation process was brutal. I was troubled that two Democratic senators, one Black and one white, each from one of two committees with jurisdiction over my position, were among the holdouts delaying my confirmation for months. Particularly biting was one Republican Senator's press release about me, entitled "America Can Do Better than This: The Case Against Lauri Fitz-Pegado." At the time, reading that document felt like a body blow.

Many within the then new Clinton administration and former colleagues on both sides of the political aisle who knew me, and knew the facts, advocated tirelessly for my confirmation on Capitol Hill and in the press. Many of the daily press inquiries and inquiries from Capitol Hill about me were fielded by my former colleague and friend at Hill and Knowlton, Cecile Ablack, who had been chosen as director of public affairs and government relations for the International Trade Administration (ITA), run by Jeff Garten, who already had been confirmed as the undersecretary of the ITA. (Jeff is the husband of Ina Garten, of *Barefoot Contessa* fame.) Cecile and Jill Schuker were relentless in their defense of me, as they also had been colleagues at Hill and Knowlton.

My confirmation was drawn out and painful to me and to my family. My son, who was a teenager at the time, awakened one morning to find a CNN crew stationed outside our suburban home. I was determined to avoid a new barrage of questions, so I exited our home through a back door. I scurried down the wooden steps, ran across the backyard, and escaped through the woods to temporary freedom. This was just one of many similar incidents that caused my family and me a great deal of pain. As I think back on that time, I am so grateful for the love and support my husband and family showed me during that deeply trying period. They provided the light that got me through those very dark days.

My sponsor and friend, Secretary Ron Brown, who had recommended my presidential nomination for the position, called me into his office toward the end of this stressful fight throughout which the Commerce Department Office of Legislative and Intergovernmental Affairs headed by Loretta Dunn, led my riddled confirmation pursuit. Her colleague, Sally Susman, diligently accompanied me to what seemed like endless meetings with senators or staff, and in which I had to repeatedly defend myself. I heard that some of my "friends" in other senior positions at Commerce, most of whom did not require confirmation, had advised the Secretary to withdraw my name from consideration. Jill, who by then had assumed the position of the Secretary's Communications Director and had helped me discover my position in the *Plum Book* (the name of a book listing political appointments for each administration) and after numerous entreaties from Ron to me to join him at Commerce, had encouraged my nomination and stood firmly in my defense.

After the exhausting, emotional roller coaster and what I believed was divided support among Clinton's

Ron and Alma Brown

Lauri's swearing in at the Department of Commerce. *From left:* Panks, Ron Brown, Fernando, Lauri, Dad, and Mom

advisors at the White House, Ron, seated at his desk in the Secretary's stately and impressive office, invited me to sit, looked me in the eyes and asked, "Fitz-a-rooni, what do you want to do, keep fighting or withdraw? I will do whatever you want." I asked for a night to sleep on it and the next day told him after consultation with my parents and a few friends that I would fight on. Ron's wife Alma also had encouraged me to hang in there when she called to tell me that she and Ron were inviting the last critical Democratic Senator who had held out, along with his wife, to dinner for a chat. Taught to always fight for what I knew to be right, to understand that I would always bear the burden of a greater level of scrutiny, and with the support of a bipartisan group of friends and former colleagues, I soon won the votes of the two committees of jurisdiction and the unusual two full Senate votes, cloture, and confirmation.

As a result of the unusual amount of time it took for my confirmation to be finalized, my swearing-in ceremony delayed the swearing in of the other three Assistant Secretary colleagues in the International Trade Administration—Ray Vickery, Chuck Meissner, and Sue Esserman. A few years later, Ray, Sue and I deeply mourned our dear colleague, Chuck Meissner, who died with Ron in that fateful plane that crashed in Dubrovnik, Croatia. My friendship with Ray and Sue only deepened after that day and has lasted through the years.

CHAPTER TEN

Revelations

nyone who has seen the 1964 painting, *The Problem We All Live With* by Norman Rockwell, should be moved. It captures brilliantly what integrating schools in this country looked like in one provocative scene: a little Black girl with her hair in pigtails adorned with a white ribbon, wearing a pristine white dress, white shoes, and white ankle socks. With upright posture and head held high, she takes a stride, clutching a notebook, escorted by four men (who appear to be white), two leading her and two bringing up the rear, clad in suits, wearing yellow arm bands which identify them as a "Deputy US Mar-

Ruby Bridges, 1955,
*photographer an
anonymous US Depart-
ment of Justice employee*

shall." In the center background of the painting is a wall with large graffiti letters spelling out the word, "NIGGER."

The little girl was Ruby Bridges, the first Black child to desegregate the all-white William Frantz Elementary School in Louisiana during the New Orleans school desegregation crisis in 1960. The ensuing decades notwithstanding, during which there was an ardent pursuit of mandated access to "equal opportunity" in education for children of color, the attempts to mix Black and white children in public-school classrooms remains an ongoing experiment whose results are, at best, questionable.

This epiphany unfolded, and embedded scar tissue surfaced, at a conference in Abu Dhabi in April 2018, when an insightful moderator of a panel on which I was to speak before an assembled audience of hundreds of artists and officials from around the world, introduced me as a metaphorical Ruby Bridges.

The panel moderator, a Syrian American journalist, lawyer, and advocate, Alia Malek, had tried to connect with me before the event; she finally caught up with me when I arrived in Abu Dhabi. I was perplexed as to why she had been so insistent about meeting and talking before the panel. I was so busy and overloaded with client work at The Livingston Group in the weeks leading up to the conference, that I was counting the days until I could board the Etihad flight and enjoy a small respite on the way to Abu Dhabi. Upon settling exhausted into my business class compartment, finally pushing back in my seat for a long-awaited uninterrupted night of sleep, my dreams of a week in the far away desert could not even come close to the life-changing experience I would soon have.

That was the moment marking the beginning of the end of my race to the finish line, the shedding of my protective armor. I never would have seen myself in Ruby, had Alia not seen me in that light and chosen to introduce me that day, in that way, in that place, to those assembled, and to me.

It was as if the moment triggered an abrupt pause in my life movie followed by a touch of the reverse arrow, when flashing across my mind were screenshots of the white and colored signs marking the water fountains at the bus rest stop as my brother Bruce and I rode the bus to Warrenton; the white robed and hooded Ku Klux Klan marching down Main Street; the tiny piece of paper where I wrote his name and hid it where I could retrieve it quickly when asked by my father to identify that famous Negro preacher who gave speeches before huge crowds of Black people, and when he finished all the people crossed arms, held hands and with bodies swaying to the rhythm sang, "We shall overcome ... black and white together ..." Little did I imagine then that it would take over 50 years before white people, mostly young, in astounding numbers, would march for real change in America, waving signs saying, "I can't breathe" and chanting "No justice, no peace" and "Black Lives Matter;" the car ride in 1968 to see the still smoldering buildings set afire by frustrated and angry Black masses in downtown DC setting their mourning afire and robbing, looting stores of things they would never have when their hope was shattered with the bullet that silenced Martin Luther King, Jr.; the trunk of the tree where the white children across the street hid, when we moved to their all-white neighborhood; the deep breath I took every day as I walked past the athletic field behind Montgomery Hills Jr. High to enter the school we Negro students integrated; the wooden bridge I crossed to catch the school bus with the Black kids to go to B-CC High School; my father on stage portraying Frederick Douglass in the play "John Brown's Body;" protesting for reforms at Vassar

and being stripped of Kendrick House, the refuge
for African American students; performing with the
Capitol Ballet at a Nixon Inaugural event; shaking
the white gloved hand of Clara Bell when I arrived
at the Santo Domingo airport for my first diplomatic
tour; understanding that even in the eyes of mostly
shades-of-brown- complexioned-Dominicans, would
believe that "indio" or any race descriptor was better
than "negro" (Black); appearing on "60 Minutes" and
the hundreds of times I attempted to tell the actual
story of representing Kuwaiti exiles, the anonymous
victims fleeing from Iraqi occupation of their country, to
the press, questioning senators, during the prolonged
confirmation process; biting my lip and holding my
tongue in countless professional meetings, social
settings, conversations with friends when unconscious
or conscious bias and outright racist comments
proliferated.

Yes, without presumption, I admitted that I, too, was
Ruby Bridges.

The reality hit me like a cold shower, shocking me from
head to toe like the electricity of a lightning bolt, leaving
my heart beating audibly but my mouth fighting to regain
its voice. I felt I was in that moment of hesitation and
doubt that often freezes you in the wings of the theater
before you step onto the stage to deliver what you have
long prepared for—a dance, a play, a speech . . . rarely had
I experienced immobility, given that I had been taught
to perform, to be comfortable before crowds, to keep my
composure, to shake it off, and I had rarely failed to deliver.

Speechless, breathing deeply and composing myself,
I embraced the revelation and let it go all at once, allowing me to find liberation and unchain my authentic
voice. I did not truly recognize nor begin to separate from

that cycle to begin my transformation until that experience in Abu Dhabi. I made the critical decision that I might be emotionally released from continuing to carry those burdens, that I had carried my weight, done my duty, and could finally breathe. My contemplation began to explore the dimensions of the change I needed to make to achieve a more authentic quality of life. That was the moment marking the beginning of the end of my dash to the elusive finish line and the beginning of living freely in my dash, in the new moment.

As a teenager, contemplating my life of ballet classes, performing with the Capitol Ballet Company, completing high school, and making critical choices about my future, the dance performance that had the greatest impact on me was Alvin Ailey's signature legacy work *Revelations*. Each expertly choreographed moment of *Revelations* burrows into places deeply embedded in my soul—those places and events that have left footprints on the ground I once walked.

Each section of *Revelations* comprises a series of masterfully executed, emotionally charged, spiritually engaging pieces danced to African American music: gospel, spirituals and blues, choreographed to reflect the spirit of powerful lyrics and music, performed in varying configurations, from solos, to the entire company. The male dancers, often slightly clad, display power, technical prowess, and graceful muscularity. The women portray strength, flawless technique, flexibility, pure lines, and emotional vulnerability. The lyrics and rhythm of the music are not only absorbed in the movements of each dancer, but they also permeate the skin of each limb, surging through the body, finding escape as glistening streams of perspiration. The range of energy and simplicity of the costuming are juxtaposed with the grandeur of the culminating pieces. The women are dressed in billowing white skirts carrying white parasols while wading in layers of magically undulating fabric. The raucous finale never fails to take the audience "to church," with the entire company dressed for worship in their Sunday finest, with the women's long flowing yellow dresses and matching bonnets with fans unfurled and poised to reduce the heat, when the spirit moves them.

After seeing it dozens of times, I still walk away grateful for having felt the breathtaking moments of heartfelt joy, excitement, sadness, and melancholy. Revelatory events throughout my life evoke the same emotions. The lyrics sometimes randomly resurface as whispers into my ear; the rhythms surge and pulse through my body, warming me into a hot or cold sweat of frustration, elation, rebellion, or resolve.

"Didn't My Lord Deliver Daniel?"

He delivered daniel from the lion's den,
jonah from the belly of the whale.
And the hebrew children from the fiery furnace,
then why not every man.

I went on my first mission trip to Cuba in 2008 with then rector Reverend Scott Benhase, a group of St. Alban's parishioners, including members, George and Beth Keys, Barbara Manard, Barbara Conyers, Susan Morris, several young people, and my daughter. Also accompanying our group was Padre Simon Bautista originally from the Dominican Republic, the Latino Missioner for our parish. My love affair with the Spanish language and Hispanic culture had begun when I was nine years old, and continued throughout high school and at Vassar, where I studied literature written by authors from Spain, Latin America, and the Caribbean. I had written my senior thesis in Spanish about the work of Cuban author Alejo Carpentier. I had lived and traveled extensively in the region, but always longed for the opportunity to visit Cuba.

I was surprised to discover one evening in Havana when talking with Barbara Conyers, a petite and perky, brown-skinned octogenarian in our delegation that she knew my mother when they had taught at the same school many years earlier. I was thrilled to later reconnect her with my mom. Barbara and I bonded quickly, and I was blessed to have her in my life. She later read a passage from the Bible at my mother's funeral.

After that trip to Cuba, Barbara accepted an invitation to be my guest at the Christmas White House tour arranged annually by the International Women's Forum. She was giddy with anticipation, sharing with me that although a longtime DC resident, she had never been to the White House. I captured in photographs her expressions of awe as she relished the beautiful decorations in each room, the aromas of pine and ginger, and sounds of a caroling high school chorus. At the commencement of these White House tours, the group congregates at one of the side gates, and then proceeds through security and into the East Wing of the White House. After the tour, guests exit through the official entrance door. Barbara asked me with a look of consternation, "Is this the front door to the White House?" I smiled with tears welling in my eyes, "Yes, Barbara, let me take a photograph of you at the front door of 1600 Pennsylvania Avenue." Slightly more than a year later, I was reminded of that moment at the service celebrating her life after she transitioned. As she journeyed toward the end of her life, she showed no glimpse of fear or regret. She was sustained by the deepest devotion and most profound faith I had ever witnessed.

Barbara, like me, was a staunch supporter of the Spanish language service at St. Alban's, which had grown out of our trip to Cuba. Although we were disappointed not to form a partnership with a church in Cuba, we were delighted that a service for our growing local Latino community was established soon thereafter at our home church. The proud, stately, devout priest, Padre Simon Bautista led that service, with his warm, beautiful Brown family attending every Sunday. I became one of the lay leaders for that congregation with the late Richard Parkins and Lynn Schmale. I continue to be a vocal advocate. The more than decade-long road to acceptance and inclusion has been rocky for both the church's majority community and its Spanish language congregation.

The Spanish language congregation has benefited from committed leadership over the past twelve years from Reverends Simon Bautista, along with Juan Pastor, Debbie Kirk, and, more recently, Emily Griffin, and Yoimel Gonzalez. Padre Simon and Reverand Debbie Kirk, a white American female priest, were particularly adept and culturally competent in serving our Latino community, in aspects well beyond leading Sunday services and providing pastoral care. Many Spanish-speaking parishioners face economic, social, and political challenges in the US, a country still struggling to address diversity and inclusion. The country struggles to develop viable policies for Brown, Black, and Asian immigrants. It seems those who are not immigrants present baffling challenges—Native Americans, those truly indigenous to the country, and descendants of enslaved Africans on whose backs this country was built. Our multicultural Spanish language service comprises members representing over a dozen countries in the Latin American and Caribbean region, sprinkled with a few white and Black parishioners striving to bridge and unify us all.

Understanding the inherent similarities, yet differences in the stories of those who emigrated and those born of enslaved peoples transported against their will to the US, is more than a nuance on our path to reconciliation. A course, Sacred Ground, has been developed in the Episcopal Church addressing the history of racism in America, and revisionist perceptions feeding discrimination, including rich theological content. For my eight fellow parishioners and me who recently walked this journey together, it was an enlightening and renewing spiritual journey. The Sacred Ground course and other inspired sermons, conferences, and conversations in the Episcopal Church are all a path to "Becoming Beloved Community." Philosopher-theologian Josiah Royce, who founded the Fellowship of Reconciliation, coined the phrase. Dr. Martin Luther King, Jr., a member of the Fellowship, referred to the concept often, giving it deeper and resonant meaning. Written in the gospel of Matthew, Chapter 8 is, ". . . now I know why I came into this world, to form God's beloved community." When we hear it in today's turbulent world, its significance is magnified. My faith and belief in these words guide me, and give me hope and strength.

During a painful period for our Spanish language members, our Rector Geoffrey Hoare invited a priest to share his experience successfully uniting and leading an English and Spanish language congregation. Among his resonant messages was that people must be willing to be uncomfortable to embrace the challenges of true unity. Discomfort is perhaps comparable to the first stage of grief. It eventually morphs into acceptance through introspection, support from others, and prayer. I am amazed at the evolution of thought and actions that is leading us to a new place of "one church, two languages." I remain hopeful that the role of religion and faith-based organizations will hasten the healing of our country.

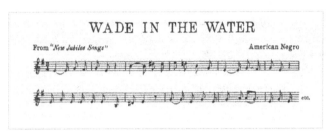

"Wade in the Water"

Wade in the water, wade in the water children
Wade in the water,
God's gonna trouble the water.

My former mentor, the late Vernon Jordan, civil rights leader, businessman, and close advisor to many including to his friend President Clinton, called me soon after the plane crash that had killed Commerce Secretary Ron Brown in April 1996. I was surprised to be tracked down in Mexico by my ever-efficient assistant Pilar Martinez. I had managed to seek refuge by the ocean in Mexico for a few days to finally escape from the suffocating gloom at the Department of Commerce as we tried futilely to return to our normal lives after what seemed to be endless funeral services of our friends and colleagues who perished in the plane crash on April 3, 1996. Pilar found me in my room where the window looked out on the side of a rocky hillside instead of the water. I was disappointed that the view was not what I anticipated or needed at that moment. I had hoped for a calming view of the ocean, but instead found the rocky hillside a menacing reminder of St. John's Mountain in Dubrovnik where the plane crashed. Any other time, I would have been outside at the beach, but I happened to be staring out that window and, in my room, when I picked up the ringing phone on the side table beside my bed. It was Pilar's voice calling from the office in DC, "Lauri, Vernon Jordan asked me to find you. I will connect him now. He said it was important."

Vernon called to ask whether I was interested in ascending to the number two position as Deputy Secretary at Commerce. During our discussion, he advised against falling into the trap of feeling compelled to finish the work of those that we had admired and lost, in lieu of defining a new path. I was honored to be considered for that position but concluded that it was time to move on. Nonetheless, I stayed at Commerce an entire year after the plane crash under the leadership of acting (temporary) Secretary Mickey Kantor and long enough to staff the next official Secretary of Commerce Bill Daley's first trip to South Africa. While I was on that trip, in Cape Town, my paternal grandfather Charles Steel Fitz died. Daley immediately let me know that I could return to the US immediately. I opted to stay. I preferred to remember Grandaddy Fitz the way I last saw him. And honestly, I wasn't yet ready to attend another funeral, particularly of a close family member, after so many funerals over that year.

I did not regret remaining at Commerce for that transitional period. However, I knew in April 1997 after working diligently on the one-year remembrance program of the fatal crash that it was time to move on. I was emotionally exhausted from my regular professional and personal responsibilities and those resulting from the losses—the weight of fulfilling the role of counselor/

psychologist, imagined on the actual shingle that read, "Assistant Secretary and Director General of the US and Foreign Commercial Service." I never imagined my next chapter would be at Iridium.

As we approached the new century, Iridium, a start-up company created by Motorola—so named because its mobile satellite phones and pagers operated within the sphere of 66 satellites, and an early competitor in the mobile, and global satellite world—was the unlikely place I landed after the Commerce Department. The year was 1997.

I experienced two CEOs at Iridium. The first, Ed Staiano, described me as "a free woman among the pseudo-free." His successor, John Richardson, said I was a street fighter. I believe that both of their perceptions of me had some merit, and each identified different dimensions of who I am. The "street" in me has served me well. It is manifested in my ability to take risks, convey confidence in the face of adversity, communicate through body language—and in my eyes there could be a warning that "you really don't want to go there with me." Those traits facilitated my ability to work well with difficult clients and individuals who are notorious for being problematic with others. They are also the source of my survival skills that have allowed me to become a proficient "code switcher," able to adapt and adjust my language, style, and delivery according to my audience. Being "multilingual" even in our own English language in this country is an asset. My street smarts aid my intuition and help place me a step ahead. I read the room, size people up quickly, and most often, accurately. These characteristics also may be at the root of why some people find me intimidating.

The street fighter comment was made by the newly board-appointed, Australian CEO John Richardson, in his office, as I anticipated being fired along with dozens of others when he took the helm of a broken public company facing a Chapter 11 bankruptcy filing. I was one of the still-standing staff members that he knew and had worked with as CEO of the Middle East and Africa gateway territories. One of my colleagues, when asked his opinion of John when he initially assumed that first role at Iridium, said he reminded him of "a character from a beach novel."

My role at the company had been somewhat of an "enforcer." With the title of head of Global Gateway Management, I was often at odds with CEOs like him. I truly expected to be a casualty of his reorganization, like many of my colleagues were, including my former Hill and Knowlton colleague John Windolph who had been well ensconced at Iridium in a senior marketing and communications role when I arrived. When I was called into the Australian's office, I was resigned to my expected fate when he surprised me by saying that he needed a street fighter like me and promptly stripped me of my previous title and redefined my responsibilities as internal and external communications. It was I who would now inform staff that they were no longer employed; it was I who would now be handling irate calls from shareholders; and, finally, it was I who would be dealing with endless press inquiries. I needed the job, so I accepted the reassignment, and drew upon my survival skills to keep moving forward.

Previously, while Ed Staiano was CEO, my team had been responsible for supporting the securing of regulatory requirements managed by investors and operators of "gateways" throughout the world. The cacophony of investors made board meetings look like the United Nations, with trustees from the major American stakeholder, Motorola, and investors in Brazil, China, Taiwan, Russia, Brazil, India, Japan, Germany, and Saudi Arabia. I had been hired to facilitate resolution of the impediments to progress within these regions with special focus on complex ownership and operations in China, the Middle East, and Africa. I had learned of the original opportunity at Iridium when Sally Painter, a colleague at Commerce, introduced me to Leo Mondale who was aware that Iridium Chairman Bob Kinzie and then CEO Ed Staiano were in search of someone with my skills. The chairman believed my background and recent experience at the Department of Commerce managing 130 global and 90 domestic offices positioned me well to work with a diverse, multicultural, group of male CEOs and investors. They managed and operated the international "gateways," and their only mutual interest was a return on their investment in a high-risk new technology. Few of those CEOs or investors with the exception of the Motorola group, were engineers, or had experience in the industry. As I saw it, the common thread binding them was making money, a sense of entitlement, their dislike of the hard charging, blunt, and critical headquarters CEO Ed Staiano, and their resentment of me: a "twofer" African American and woman who, at the instruction of Staiano, was, simply put, riding herd on them.

Adding insult to injury was my staff of technically competent and language-proficient men and women, familiar with their country/regions of responsibility. Their job responsibilities included regular deployment to their respective assigned territories to support and assist the local CEO with the regulatory approval process to secure the required licenses and permits for Iridium to operate in each country of their region. In many countries of the world at the end of the century, there was no regulatory framework or responsible institution. "Challenging" was an understatement for my staff and my colleague Francis Latapie's staff, all based at Iridium's corporate headquarters in Washington, DC, with homes on airplanes and in hotel rooms around the globe. Our frequent presence to assist in these countries—in person and on the ground as mandated by Staiano—was seen as an intrusion by some of the gateway leadership. In the eyes of CEO Staiano, many of the countries/regions were behind schedule and underperforming. He designed a chart of green, yellow, and red racing cars as a report card on their status, which he boldly unveiled at board meetings. Those trailing in the race were disclosed before their competitive fellow trustees and senior Iridium headquarters staff. All the regional CEOs, who were later confronted by their respective trustees, disdained the racing car imagery. Even after the daunting but successful task of launching the required low earth orbit satellites and securing sufficient country permits, the company was failing and Staiano was out. Soon, one of the former drivers of the often lagging red and yellow racing cars ascended to the CEO throne and had the opportunity to seek his revenge.

I felt that the description of me as "free," by Staiano, a former Motorola senior executive, who was an experienced and respected engineer and avowed fitness fanatic, was in keeping with the "street fighter" metaphor as well. He and I clearly had different definitions of freedom. Perhaps his perception was a relative definition when assessing a woman and an African American. Whatever his rationale, in his eyes I embodied what he needed for support: a strong individual willing to carry his water and push progress to meet his rigorous expectations. He saw quickly that I could perform this task under highly intimidating circumstances, branding me perhaps as an uncharacteristically liberated, atypical female in the male-dominated world of engineers. He may have viewed me as free, but I did not feel, recognize, or embrace my freedom until two decades later.

As fate would have it, I was among the last to turn

off the lights at Iridium headquarters. Soon after leaving that chapter behind, I stumbled across a briefing by Reverend Jesse Jackson upon his return from a telecom business mission trip to Africa. One of the businessmen in his delegation had become interested in investing in, and rebuilding, Iridium. Just as many of us at Iridium envisioned, had the business plan worked and the technology cooperated, African nations would be able to leapfrog over cellular directly to mobile satellite telecommunications access in the rural and remote areas of countries that suffered with limited telecom access and even worse infrastructure. That businessman believed strongly that Iridium could be reinvented to prioritize a developing world landscape. After I left Iridium, I became an independent consultant, and he became my first client. And, indeed, he soon became an investor in the successful next iteration of Iridium.

"Oh, Sinner, You'd Better Get Ready"

Oh, sinnerman, where you gonna run to?
Oh, sinnerman where you gonna run to?
Where you gonna run to? All on that day.

A principal at Gray told me for the first, but not only time in my life, that he thought of me as white. I was the only professional of color there at the time and one of very few that worked at Gray and Company during my decade-plus years of employment there. I have heard others utter the equally cringe-worthy comment, that they don't see color when they engage with me. I know it is intended as the highest compliment, but I often wonder if the white people who make these comments ever wonder what the person of color on the receiving end of the conversation thinks when they hear it. Of course, it is probably the belief of those in the majority community who make these inane comments, that this is a fair standard they can eagerly apply to those of us who are achievers, well credentialed, capable, and, most importantly, resilient. They reserve these seemingly positive comments for those who defy stereotypes and preconceived notions of race, color, gender, and abilities. What they don't realize is how narrow minded they are to view us through the eyes of the traditional and still-dominant power dynamic. Their well-intentioned comments, often spoken as if after a light bulb breakthrough realization, are in the family of inappropriate old-school "compliments" that include the ridiculous and sophomoric, "You are a credit to your race." These people would be surprised to learn that those of us who successfully and even impressively navigate their space, insist that they see us in all our vibrant color. For we are rarely allowed to forget that we are indeed people of color when every morning we gaze upon our reflection in the mirror.

"Morning and Evening"

Lord, keep us safe this night. Secure from all our fears.
May angels guard us while we sleep.
Till morning light appears.

I led a workshop on the role of art in underserved, or as we rebranded them, resilient communities at the "Cultural Conference 2018" in Abu Dhabi. The theme was "Unexpected Collaborations." I also participated on a panel focused on the same subject whose members hailed from diverse geographic and professional spaces. The conference comprised a global space of artists and ministers of culture and tourism from over forty countries engaged in performances, impromptu jam sessions, and wondrous conversations. There were many unexpected pairings of artists—a cellist from Iran with a dancer from India who had not previously met, and who produced magical moments of artistry born out of the equivalent of what could be classified as speed dating.

It was serendipitous that the Marvel movie *Black Panther* had recently debuted in the US starring the late Chadwick Boseman, an unprecedented Black superhero in a story populated with Black actors. I talked about its significance to African Americans, its popularity with whites, and its global appeal. While I explained it as a seminal cultural milestone and social commentary in nearby Saudi Arabia, people were standing in line to view the first movie shown in the country in thirty-five years.

I was invited to participate in the conference by David Rothkopf, a former colleague at the Commerce Department who had secured a contract from the Abu Dhabi government to organize the event. His assistant on this project was a mentee, Stacie Williams, a former professional dancer reinventing herself in the world of international affairs after graduating from the Georgetown School of Foreign Service. Stacie and I had met in an adult ballet class at The Washington School of Ballet, taught by the gifted instructor, coach, and choreographer, Aaron Jackson. I have developed deep and abiding friendships with several of my adult ballet classmates and instructors.

Among my unexpected Abu Dhabi-born collaborations that arose is one with Dutch artist and designer, Jeroen Koolhaas. There, at the new Louvre Abu Dhabi—a stunning sight to behold—Jeroen and his cofounder of Favela Painting, Dre Urhahn, spoke of their experiences in resilient neighborhoods in various countries, several in places with which I shared a deep connection, including Brazil, Haiti, Curaçao, and the inner cities of the US. Their immersive experiences were novel and genuine, and Jeroen's apparent comfort in the favelas, despite being a white man from a country notoriously mired in a history of colonialism and slavery, opened in me a fascination and curiosity.

Jeroen and I discovered our uncanny connection on the afternoon of the last day of the conference while relaxing at the hotel rooftop poolside. The conference organizers had left the attendees with an unstructured afternoon to relax before most of our flights departed for our homes in the far corners of the globe. Over the course of a marathon evening of discussion, during our

Brazilian women in Rio creating tile work, *photographer Andrew Lenz*

last hours in Abu Dhabi, the two of us engaged in a candid and extremely revealing conversation. We became like seatmates on a very long flight, who after getting as comfortable as possible in our respective seats, at first, only exchanged pleasantries but soon engaged in unencumbered conversation with a stranger you assumed you would never see again. Over those many hours, Jeroen and I shared information with each other that we would never disclose even to a best friend.

That initial in-person dialogue continued later as a virtual conversation as we explored our backgrounds, beliefs, influences, and potential creative collaborations—beginning with to cowrite a screenplay, an ambitious first collaboration. Since that seminal afternoon and evening in Abu Dhabi, we have been engaged in a journey designed to share with US audiences the experiences and successful models for creating inclusive, community-based art. With the objective of expanding Jeroen's footprint in the United States, we have sought to communicate the lessons learned from his work of building community through art. Based on successful models in multiple countries, he and his collaborators have engaged

Milk. *Portrait by Jeroen Koolhaas, courtesy of the artist*

fully, living in the communities they feature for weeks and months at a time. In these underserved and resilient communities, they teach and employ neighborhood residents to rebrand the associated negative stereotypes with images and designs on buildings and streets reflecting the strength, hope, and beauty of these enclaves. This vision has evolved as we explore projects designed to use art as a creative vehicle for social change—in education, economic development and exposure to multiculturalism, and in an attempt to transform individuals, communities, and public perception.

Jeroen's early education and creative thought were uniquely informed by exposure to all genres of music and an understanding of world events—blues, jazz, the civil rights movement, opera, the history of colonialism, music of protest, soul music, the antiapartheid movement, reggae, samba, and hip-hop. His knowledge about, and love of, music has led him to become a well-known DJ, which has further influenced his art. He has incorporated and reflected in his work, music, math, architecture, textiles, and color. He captures the traditional, literal, and modern in his designs, murals, abstract art, and portraits. My experience in cultural diplomacy and dance complements his experience, as do our language

Koolhaas and team in front of Denver mural. *From left:* Lauri, two artists from Philadelphia, artist from Brazil, and Jeroen, *photographer Andrew Lenz*

skills, travels, contrasting heritages, generational span, and genders.

Jeroen and I also share a deep commitment to inclusion and to maintaining relationships with people we have met and valued on our respective global journeys. We had the opportunity to bring four individuals with whom he had worked, two from Brazil and two from North Philly, to participate in a mural commission in Denver. I was familiar with his capacity to produce impressive artwork, but what I marveled at was our intercultural experience and his cultural competence, his innate ability to relate to people from all walks of life, and to be able to create an environment for them that provided comfort and purpose.

I, from my own perspective, also see the versatility and range of his work as comparable to that of a dancer's. He is grounded in classical technique but versatile and flexible, capable of applying core technique and training to different dance genres—modern, jazz, contemporary, hip-hop, and ballroom. Jeroen is as nimble and as flexible as a dancer, whether performing and creating on the stage, a wall, a building, or the canvas of the creative mind.

"I Want to Be Ready"

I want to be ready, Lord
Ready to put on my long white robe.

I became a very early supporter of Barack Obama's campaign for president. I wondered what kind of relationship Obama and Ron Brown would have had. I met Senator Barack Obama when at TLG I took my client, a board member of the South African chemical company Sasol, to meet with the junior Senator from Illinois on the Foreign Relations Committee. Securing that appointment was not difficult because the board member was Max Sisulu, son of revered Mandela prison mate and ANC leader, Walter Sisulu. Senator Obama was honored to meet him, and the conversation was warm and significant for both, and meaningful to me as well, contributing to my positive impression of Obama. I assisted Susan Rice to organize one of Obama's early fund-raisers in the summer of 2007 in DC. Earlier in January 2007 my daughter Briana and I joined the team on the ground in cold, snowy Keene, New Hampshire, spending days knocking on doors and phone banking from sunup to sundown, grabbing dinner at Applebee's with our group from DC—Susan Rice and her son Jake, Esther Brimmer, who became Assistant Secretary of State for International Organizations, with her husband Steven Beller, and son Nathaniel. (The boys attended Maret School, a few classes behind Briana, and Nathaniel followed Briana's example of graduating from the University of Edinburgh and living in the UK.)

We all believed our children should experience the history of the moment and were ecstatic when Obama won the critical first Iowa Caucus, marking the win in detail in his memoir as the turning point in his campaign; the moment the possibility of the presidency became real. He was as gracious as he had been in the meeting with Max Sisulu when he gathered us four days later to thank us all after his disappointing primary loss to Hillary Clinton in New Hampshire. Despite that loss, I remained, in the words of Emily Chiles "fired up" and "ready to go." This became the catchy campaign call and response for the remainder of his campaign, during fund-raising, phone banking, getting out the vote in Pennsylvania and Virginia—particularly in Latino communities where my Spanish was useful—and poll watching on election day.

I heard major skepticism and outright assertions that Obama could never win to become the first Black president of the US, both from politically astute friends here in the US and many abroad. I remember the sting of a client's words at dinner in London with my colleague at TLG and friend Duane Gibson. This corporate executive and former UK diplomat said, "He won't become president. He has never even been to Europe." After dinner that evening, I went to a pub, plugged in my earphones, and listened to Obama's historic speech about race in

America and his run for president. Those words coming from an African American man, who I believed would become president of the United States, drove me to tears as I listened, and with my glass of Pinot noir I silently toasted in my mind each poignant word. I was in the company of very few Obama supporters in my TLG office. I proudly displayed a poster-sized photo of Obama on the cover of *Jet Magazine*, conveying that unique Blackman-swagger laced with the requisite confidence. On occasion when Mark Lindsay, a Democrat and former White House advisor to President Clinton and consultant to TLG, stopped by my office, we had those conversations that you can have only with those who have shared your life experiences. I welcomed those moments. Mark, an African American from Cleveland who staffed the late, great Representative Lou Stokes, and Duane Gibson, a conservative white Republican, are good friends dating back to their law school days together. Their friendship is a testament to our ability to bridge partisanship and mitigate vitriol through mutual respect, conversation, and relationship building.

I was so grateful to receive from Bob Livingston tickets that he did not plan to use for reserved seating at Barack Obama's Inaugural swearing-in ceremony. I took my dad and Briana to the historic event on that frigid January 20th. I had served in government twice before Obama was elected, and I would have gone back a third time, should I have been asked to join his administration. I knew, unfortunately, that was not possible given his campaign pledge restricting lobbyists from serving. That never deterred my commitment and the echoing in my ear of the energizing campaign chant, "Yes, we can."

CHAPTER ELEVEN

Coda

A "coda" is the last movement of a group of dancers, or the finale of a pas de deux in a ballet. Upon returning to Washington after my trip to Abu Dhabi, encouraged by my wise friend Merianne de Merode, I took a leap of faith and met with her visiting friend and healer Vardit, a petite Israeli woman. The experience was seminal from so many perspectives. Under Vardit's watchful eyes and with a mesmerizing tone, she transported me to a past where I found myself trapped and shackled on a slave ship trying desperately to break free. As she led me through a process of perceived physical and emotional liberation, I broke the chains and emerged from that regression, feeling an unprecedented lightness and sense of freedom. I continued the awakening I had begun in Abu Dhabi, when I was introduced as a metaphorical Ruby Bridges and was taken to the next level. Vardit observed with uncanny insight that this moment was likely the first time in my life that I was experiencing true liberation. She explained that I had been stifled and compromised professionally and personally, and that perhaps now that I had allowed myself to break free through this process, I could pursue an unfettered future. This was the first time I had experienced anything like this exploration of the subconscious. The result was a palpable emotional release, a feeling of relief. It was not something I ordinarily would have opened my mind to or embraced. Since that session, I have become intentional about how I expend my time, attention, and energy.

I soon ended a four-decade-long full-time professional career—no more interrupted nights ridden with client calls, emails, and texts. My new dreams were filled with images of Santibáñez, Spain, the town I had visited with Santiago and his family, with fields of giant sunflowers, the tall yellow-petaled flowers with dark seeds forming a circle in the center, dancing in the breeze, spreading as far as the eye can see. I longed to return to that town where I knew I would find calm, gentle warmth, and peace. I called Santiago, who I had met in Spain when he was a curious seventeen-year-old boy and I, a wide-eyed seventeen-year-old-girl. I told him that I longed for our talks, shared memories, and our strolls on paths along the sunflower fields. He simply asked, "When shall I pick you up at the Madrid airport? We will drive straight to wherever you want to go, 'dondequiera (wherever).'" That unconditional relationship grows more precious with time.

I stopped simply contemplating an overdue life change and turned the corner, leaving behind that long-term career, reassessing my many "volunteer" commitments, family responsibilities, and personal relationships, engendering consternation and concern from some and admiration from others.

I was able to restructure my life, filling it with things I wanted to do with people I wanted to share time, which assumed a new value. It was liberating. I find comfort and purpose as I engage in projects with the potential to contribute to social justice, systemic and structural change, engaging in constructive dialogue about actions to address critical issues facing our nation and the world, supporting institutions, organizations, and people of like mind, values, and creative pursuits consistent with these aesthetics. I admit that I have not completely broken the habit of overbooking and over committing myself. However, reengaging in an occasional hundred-yard dash is now a choice, not a necessity.

As a rare native Washingtonian, I have observed and experienced the transformation, gentrification, and modernization of my city. DC has been called the most gentrified city in the country, a fact engendering mixed emotions. I understand that development, growth, renovating, and improving neighborhoods will occur in major urban areas, and that there are advantages to some along the way. The displacement of communities, changes in demographics, the complexion of the new communities from black to white, raise age-old issues about who the beneficiaries and victims are. One advantage of these shifts has for some been the growth and diversity of creative communities. Washington, DC, has attracted an unprecedented number of ballet instructors of color teaching children of color at various dance institutions in the city.

This has inspired The Collective (TC), comprising ballet instructors and managers of dance institutions of color dedicated to ballet training, and the growth and development of children of color. TC's members have decades of dance experience navigating and excelling in a world historically challenged with issues of opportunity, equity, and inclusion of underrepresented artists, managers, and administrators.

Following is a compilation of the current members' backgrounds as well as some of their views concerning The Collective established in 2019.

- Sandra Fortune-Green, cofounder of The Collective and artistic director of the Jones-Haywood Dance School, has a distinguished ballet career described earlier in Chapter Two, "*Agon*." Sandra, with fifty years of teaching experience, continues as a ballet instructor at both Jones-Haywood and the Duke Ellington School of the Arts.

- Kahina Haynes, Executive Director, Dance Institute of Washington (DIW), began her dance training with her grandmother, continued at the Maryland Youth Ballet and the School of American Ballet. She has a B.A. from Princeton University and a Master's Degree from Oxford University in Evidence Based Social Intervention. She has worked in program and process evaluation for nonprofits and international organizations. Kahina assumed leadership of DIW after the sudden loss of its founder, former dancer Fabian Barnes. Kahina has applied her dance, academic, and analytical acumen to the commendable development of DIW, a community-based, holistic dance school for children of color.

- Monica Stephenson, Director of The Washington Ballet School at THEARC (SE Campus), is from Fayetteville, NC, trained at the University of North Carolina School of the Arts and the Houston Ballet Academy; performed professionally with The Washington Ballet, Dance Theatre of Harlem Ensemble, and Los Angeles Ballet before completing her Master of Arts in Dance Education at New York University.

- Adrian Vincent James and I met when we were teenagers at the George Washington University Workshop for Careers in the Arts where several of us from Jones-Haywood who shared that summer experience encouraged him to join us at Jones-Haywood to study and dance with the Capitol Ballet. He became our colleague for several years before earning a B.F.A. in Drama with a concentration in Directing from Howard University and an M.A. in Performing Arts-Dance from the American University. He was the first African

American dancer of the Houston Ballet and teaches ballet at the Duke Ellington School of the Arts. Adrian said, "Belonging to The Collective, I am a part of something bigger and more important than myself, able to share my perspective as an African American ballet artist to shape young African American dancers for the future."

- Royce Zackery is associate professor, head coordinator of Howard University Dance Arts Program. He is an NYU Steinhardt/American Ballet Theatre alumnus and Southern Methodist University graduate, "fortunate enough to travel the world bringing joy, inspiration, and education." Returning to full performance health after a paralyzing injury, he said, "opened my mind, body, and spirit to a greater calling in teaching. The personal journey of daily failures combined with weekly triumphs lay foundations in wisdom of how not only to be successful, but efficiently effective." Royce sees the group "filled with artistic and scholastic greatness expanding 4 generations of brilliance. I am honored to stand alongside this phenomenal group of people dedicated to service and community, giving back to the art form that has given us all so much."

- Stacie Williams, teaching at Jones-Haywood, with a day job in international affairs after returning from her career at Dance Theatre of Harlem stated, "It is an honor to be a founding member of The Collective. It provides a unique opportunity for both fellowship with other ballet teachers of color, and a platform to serve the unique needs of our young ballet students of color. I have learned so much from my fellow instructors since The Collective's inception and continue to be inspired by their generosity of spirit and excellence in teaching and mentoring."

- Damien Johnson, ballet instructor at The Washington Ballet's THEARC and at Jones-Haywood, is from Texas, danced with London's Ballet Black, the Dance Theatre of Harlem, and the Los Angeles Ballet.

The Collective is founded on the principle that effective change of the current ballet paradigm requires skills intrinsic to those who have developed requisite *cultural competence* through personal journeys. Ballet training instills in youth enduring skills, applicable to critical personal and professional sustainability in and outside of the creative sector. Children of color in environments grappling with systemic racism require instructors, role models, and mentors experienced in overcoming such formidable, but not insurmountable, challenges. Recent and tragic physical health, and mental health, economic and social justice currents have exacerbated these challenges.

We in TC organize opportunities for our students from local dance institutions to meet on familiar ground, in the ballet studio, taught by renowned guest instructors. These instructors not only teach enriching master classes but also engage in candid discussion with students, their parents, and other instructors about the life of a dancer of color. We approach our work recognizing that few will reach the acclaim of these role models, but nevertheless, ensuring that all our students will reap the lifetime benefits of the critical skill sets they inevitably will require along the way.

It is crucial for parents of aspiring dancers to understand what is required of them to support their children's rigorous and demanding training. Instructors who collaborate can share information, learn from each other, and find mutual support when walls of competition are eliminated. Parents and students benefit from opportunities to meet and engage with those who can advise families about complex decisions.

At an International Women's Forum event in Annapolis, I met Gail Letts and discovered that we shared an acquaintance with Donna Ransone, who was a board member of the Richmond Ballet. Donna and Gail arranged a tour and meeting with senior staff of the Richmond Ballet School in the fall of 2018 at the time of their 35th Anniversary Gala. I was impressed with the physical structure, curriculum, and staff at the school, as well as the longtime Artistic Director Stoner Winslett, of this relatively small and impressive ballet company. Their successful program to introduce movement and dance to students in underserved Richmond communities resulted in several of the predominantly young students of color from the program becoming students at the ballet school, developing into apprentices, and ultimately becoming performing members of the Richmond Ballet. The unexpected diversity of the programs and company are a tribute to Winslett's prescient vision. Winslett, a white woman from the South who has witnessed the enduring strength of racism in the arts, has not accepted the exclusion of talented diverse dancers from her school or company. She has achieved this in the heart of the capital city of a state still struggling with redressing its history with racism. Her example inspired me to study her model so that her best practices might be a guiding light for others.

I also visited Canada's National Ballet School in Toronto during an International Women's Forum conference. It has an impressive ballet school and academic program for boarding students. What resonated equally with me were its major outreach programs for local communities of all ages and backgrounds in Toronto and in the provinces with a mandate to "share the transformative power of dance." I now have connected their school with TC. We are collaborating on several projects promoting the benefits of culture and creative perspectives to expand minds and improve relationships–elements essential to progress and positive change.

It is gratifying to see the growth of organizations, dance schools, and current and former dance artists who communicate the rich history artists of color have made to the field of dance. The Washington, DC, headquartered International Association of Blacks in Dance (IABD), led by president and CEO Denise Saunders Jones, is critical to the preservation of the past and future of Black dance, to educating the world about the history and unheralded contributions of Blacks in dance, and to facilitating opportunities for aspiring Black dancers. It has pioneered education, international conferences, funding, advocacy, and support for all those engaged in dimensions of dance grounded in the African tradition and involving the African Diaspora. Instrumental to the creation and establishment of IABD in 1988 and its hallmark conferences are Joan Myers Brown, (the Philadelphia Dance Company, Philadanco), Cleo Parker Robinson (Cleo Parker Robinson Dance), Jeraldyne Blunden (Dayton Contemporary Dance Company), Lula Washington (Lula Washington Dance Theatre), and Ann Wiliams (Dallas Black Dance Theatre). Carol Foster, a friend who joined Joyce Mosso Stokes and me in leading the Jones Haywood Alumni Association, has long invested in institutions and dancers at IABD and beyond. Carol has a degree in arts administration, credentials that are often inadequate at dance companies and schools. Carol has dedicated countless hours to supporting arts institutions, developing plans to address crises, and guiding the recovery of many challenged dance institutions.

MOBBallet (Memoirs of Blacks in Ballet), established in 2015 by Teresa Ruth Howard, was created to "... illuminate the lesser-known history and legacies of international professional Black ballet artists that have been muted, or oftentimes eradicated from the larger canon of dance ... " Her focus on these stories is timely as the majority dance world struggles to understand how and whether to create policies and practices to rectify inequities and lack of inclusion of dancers of color.

I find purpose in contributing to the growth of inclusion, recognition of diverse talent, underserved communities, and strengthening of supportive institutions. I believe in the the power of art to instill life skills in children and the resonant voices of the creative sector summoning a revolution of thought and practice.

We are advised to attain balance in our lives. I learned the tenets of achieving balance in ballet with more proficiency than achieving balance in life. I understood more clearly what was required to find balance without the support of the barre in ballet class. Dancers are expected to balance on one leg, jump and land on one leg, pirouette on one leg, requiring proper body alignment, strength, and focus. Developing balance begins early in ballet training, at the barre, with exercises facing one direction while supporting the body with one hand gently placed on the barre, then turning to the other side and repeating it with the other hand on the barre. At the end of the exercise, most often there is a requirement to hold a position without the support of the barre. The instructor says, "now balance," and you must sustain the position for several seconds. It is a test. Should you be successful at mastering exercises at the barre and the ability to balance for increasingly more seconds, you are expected to carry over those skills into the center floor where there is no barre and where you are taught to combine movements and begin to integrate elements to learn the steps/choreography and to perform.

Ironically, with time, experience, and wisdom, I learned that unlike in ballet, I could not achieve balance in my life by strength alone. I was neither invincible nor indispensable. Being vulnerable, off balance at times, asking for support, admitting to weaknesses, and knowing my limitations and myself became essential.

These new engagements, focus, and dedication to pursuits I believe in have prepared me for our country's tumultuous political times. I have recognized two important results of what is happening—the exposure of entrenched views and an increased opportunity for difficult conversations. My life experiences have informed my gift to serve as a bridge, to recognize my privilege but not lose sight of my responsibility, to not be a spectator but to be fully engaged and embrace my capacity to lead.

I am driven to support dancers who too often are plagued by injury, fatigue, abbreviated careers, or a decision to abandon the spotlight for an alternative career. COVID-19 has devastated many communities, including the dance world. Financial cushion is not in most artists' vocabulary. Dancers rarely prioritize finances above passion for their art. When facing a debilitating injury, the need or choice to transition from dance to another profession, many struggle to make a living. The younger ones may transform themselves to become competitive in a completely new job market, while the older ones are lucky if they find employment as dance teachers, or as artistic directors in a limited number of positions at dance schools and companies. Those of color have been grossly underrepresented in major companies, their associated schools, or the executive offices. The rigorous development and performance abilities of dancers have been researched and found to qualify them as master athletes. Is it not time to afford them equivalent compensation, treatment, and recognition?

Dancers are the athletes of God.

—Albert Einstein

Just when I was relishing my new life rhythm, all was disrupted in our nation and across the globe in 2020. Devastating the world indiscriminately, the COVID-19 pandemic descended on what little peace and predictability we knew. In addition, the virus has not been so equitable in selecting its victims and has instead disproportionately attacked our Black and Brown communities in the US with profound economic, social, and emotional consequences. A high percentage of our service sector employees are on the front lines of our workforce, and although African Americans and Latinos disproportionately comprise essential workers in many communities, access to affordable health care, housing, and education remain out of reach for them. So, while the entire country was forced to pause and "shelter in place" to contain the pandemic, Americans were also forced to see what they had chosen to ignore—the consequences of the continuing inequities rampant in our country.

As we struggled to cope with the COVID-19 crisis, the surging numbers of deaths and infected in the US and around the world, the unprecedented soaring unemployment, and changing protocols to combat the virus daily, suddenly the breaking news was no longer graphs, statistics, and curves related to an unpredictable, invisible virus. All of America, trapped in their COVID-19 cocoons, saw a video that shifted the narrative to the indisputably visible—a video of what had been happening for four hundred years in one form or another, but now had a captive audience unable to avoid the images, to deny that it happened, or to have anywhere to go to get away, to find refuge from the horrific scene of George Floyd, a Black man pleading for his life with his last breath as it was being snuffed out under the knee of a usurping authority figure. America was drowning under yet another moment of truth, and finally, no one else could breathe, and so they took to the streets in protest. The death of yet another Black victim of institutional and systemic racism was laid bare. It resonated with those who had previously been able to remain blind to the inequities, the disparities, and the fragility of our humanity. Perhaps the timeliness of the virus weakened our nation's and the world's immunity to the disease of denial.

These dual pandemics, COVID-19 and racism, have challenged everyone and everything over which many believed they had dominion. It demanded of us responses and solutions found only in the depths of our minds, bodies, and souls. It exposed us, stripped us of power and posturing, and led us to explore our prejudice and privilege. We were surprised to see how those we believed we knew appeared in their nakedness. Feelings we had never allowed to surface had emerged—raw, unfettered, and unapologetic.

At the core of discrimination of all types is the disease of bias—whether conscious or unconscious—entitlement, lack of exposure, and ignorance. Embracing the inclusion of those of another race, ethnicity, class, gender, ability or tribe, requires discomfort, and a desire to acquire cultural competence and courage. However, a somewhat marginally effective treatment has so far been applied to the pandemic of racism, as it dissolves into temporary periods of remission, with the cure seemingly still in experimental stages, and with more placebos than effective drugs.

The new loudest voices raised in protest, replacing those of the 1968 demonstrations and riots, are distinctly different; they are inclusive, not only Black and Brown but also young and white Indigenous, and Asian American and Pacific Islanders. Consequently, leaders are emerging from unexpected places and uncomfortable conversations are encouraged rather than avoided. Finally, change has a chance like never before.

During a crisis, the capacity of artists to remain agile and adaptable is endless. The nature of creativity always has thrived even in the most-dire circumstances. The characteristics artists inherently have or develop include discipline, flexibility, and the ability to design creative solutions. These abilities, physical and mental, are sustaining and provide strength not only to allow the artist to persevere but to flourish and identify alternative ways to train and perform.

Black Lives Matter sign

Protestors in front of Sidwell Friends School, Washington, DC

Dancers have survived the unexpected tragedy of the pandemic innovatively. They have continued their training, sought and designed safe performance venues showcasing adaptive choreography, and are compliant with health protocols. The creative sector is definitionally resilient, circumventing limitations and leading innovation.

My love affair with dance has sustained me, given me strength, and has been a lifelong guiding force propelling me to summit many mountains. Finally, I am the master of the dance "in my dash." I now can select the music, movement, venue, choreographer, principala, corps de ballet, and even the audience.

I learned that discipline is not negotiable, grace is a consequence of humility, devotion to something greater than oneself is salvation . . .

—Toni Bentley
Australian American dancer and writer

I have been blessed with a "space for grace" in my life. This gift is rooted in my faith. With much prayer and reflection, I also have learned the importance of forgiving others, and of forgiving myself.

Space for grace created a sense of safety that extended an invitation to share both one's beauty and one's brokenness with boldness. Naming and claiming the totality of one's being is a modeling of boldness that can reap many benefits healing and growth.

I believe that everyone has a fervent desire to be heard, seen, loved, and connected. I also believe that these fervent desires are typically fervently kept secret because of our need to honor our projected image to others rather than being honest with the reality of who we really are. Intentionally infusing a space for grace into our conversations as we develop healthy relationships with each other enables a realization that whatever situation in which we find ourselves, we're not in it alone.

—The Rev. Dr. Robert T. Phillips,
senior associate for Leadership Development
and Congregational Care,
Episcopal Diocese of Washington

Reverence

At the end of a ballet class, the pianist plays an adagio often laced with dramatic runs. Traditionally, the class executes slow, lyrical movements concluding in a curtsy by the females and a bow by the males as a gesture of respect and gratitude to the instructor and the pianist. The ballet term for this closing ritual is a *reverence*.

I have honored, paid homage to, thanked, and acknowledged many throughout this story. However, many organizations, associations, institutions and groups of friends and supporters have influenced me.

My most highly valued relationships have been enduring. I have concentric circles of friends, and I prefer to savor my relationships within each circle independently. I am known to have an unusually vast network and an ability to access and connect people. My opinion and support are sought by many and has led them to job opportunities, averting disasters, expanding contacts, and new friendships. I have benefitted from mentors and sponsors who have provided sage counsel when I have needed it most. Understanding that value, I have allowed mentoring to be a priority, supporting my goal to

Vassar reunion. 2018. *From left:* Jennifer Jones
'77, Paula Williams Madison '74, and Patricia
James Jordan '72

"give back" and to stay in touch with our future leaders.

My friendships with parishioners at St. Albans have grown and sustained me spiritually in my professional life over the past fifteen years. My engagement began with the gift that church participation brought to Briana and has extended to serving on our Vestry. I continue to participate in meetings of Downtown Workers' Lunch with the Rector so ably organized by John Daniel Reaves, even though I joined the group when I was at The Livingston Group for the spiritual support it provided, when I joined fellow parishioners experiencing similar professional challenges. As a member of the Global Mission Committee, we support schools in DC, South Sudan and Jordan. I find being on the board of Workers of St. Alban's fulfilling and aligned with my grounding in racial and social justice work. St. Alban's proceeds from our secondhand Opportunity Shop are disseminated as grants to Washington area nonprofit organizations.

I remain close to many friends from Vassar. Several of us remain in regular contact, including classmate Jennifer Jones, Karen Turner (attorney and a recent first time author); LaFleur Paysour, whose shoes, even before construction began, were powdered with the clay of the Smithsonian National Museum of African American

History and Culture; and Beatrix (Trixie) Fields, who attended and supported Jones-Haywood School of Ballet and still lives in the neighborhood. We renew those relationships with alumni and current students of color through an on-campus organization, the African American Alumni Association (Triple AVC), established in the 1980s that honors the legacy of commitment to our ideals. We formally come together for a weekend program on the campus every three years. The perpetual beauty of the Vassar campus, the memories it invokes, the depth and breadth of the issues we explore, and the profound strength of community comprise our bond, and preserve the legacy. No meeting concludes without a good 'ole school dance party, usually led by the most senior women among us, often to the astoundment of the newcomers who are amazed that we still *got moves*.

Among my "girl groups" is my "dysfunctional" book club, so named because we have shared many great evenings, some of which focused more on politics, fantastic food and drink, and our lives than on talk about books. We're a collection of high-level, notable Washington insiders, all politically engaged, with experience as former high-ranking government and private sector leaders, academics and policy wonks; there is virtually no one that one of our circles cannot reach through no more than three degrees of separation, rather than six. The book club comprises a group of women, many perhaps undervalued in Washington, DC's overcrowded and often insular political circles.

Our book club (including current and former) members:

- Jill Schuker, founder of our group, former Carter and Clinton administration official, public affairs executive, Head of Center, Organization for Economic Cooperation and Development (OECD), Godmother of two and affectionately called "Abu" (short for abuela "grandmother" in Spanish) to their three children.

From left: Jill Schuker, Aunt Margaret, and Margot Wilson, *photographer Milton Williams*

- Margot Wilson, Department of Energy in the Carter administration, ran for Congress in Boston, avid supporter and volunteer for Barack Obama's presidential campaigns, ranked by the *Wall Street Journal* in the top 200 in real estate, lawyer, and mother extraordinaire of four.
- Paula Stern, international trade specialist, spouse, and proud mother of two and grandmother, former chair of the International Trade Commission, businesswoman, and prolific sculptor, shares my passion for dance, occasionally joining me at adult ballet classes.
- Jane Bandler, school guidance counselor, Foreign Service spouse of Ambassador Don Bandler, supporter of Foreign Service families. Her family befriended my daughter Lwena when the Bandlers were assigned to Embassy Paris and our daughters Lara and Lwena (studying at the American University of Paris) were contemporaries.
- Christine Varney, friend since she worked for Chairman Ron Brown at the Democratic National Committee (DNC), colleagues at the Clinton-Gore Inaugural Committee, Clinton White House Secretary to the Cabinet, Federal Trade Commissioner, Obama administration Assistant Attorney General for the Antitrust Division, spouse, and mother of two.
- Aviva Meyer, Middle East specialist, New Israel Fund,

Americans for Peace Now, organizer of visits to the Middle East and Turkey, advocate for peace.

- Anne Luzzatto, Clinton administration official at Department of Commerce, Office of the US Trade representative, program director Council on Foreign Relations, President's Committee on the Arts (Obama), photographer.
- Anne Fleming, real estate, longtime politico and activist in Washington, DC, wife of broadcast journalist Gordon Peterson.
- Nancy Rubin, Clinton administration US Ambassador to the United Nations Commission on Human Rights, Trustee of the National Democratic Institute, first chair of the National Mental Health Awareness Campaign, Chair of Adopt-A-Minefield, Board of Didi Hirsch Mental Health Services, named for her mother.
- Myra Moffett, attorney, artist, campaign volunteer for Democratic candidates, at state and federal levels, wife of former congressman Toby Moffett, lay reader at St. Alban's, mother and grandmother of five children and several grandchildren, and who welcomes many into her embrace.
- Peggy Hamburg, former New York Public Health Commissioner, Director of the Food and Drug Administration (Obama administration), medical doctor, wife and mother of two. As a testament to my customary patter of three degrees of separation and not the normal six, in a random conversation, I learned that Peggy's late mother Beatrix A. Hamburg, was the first African American student to attend Vassar who did not pass for white. She went on to become the first African American woman to attend Yale Medical School. We, a few DC-based Black Vassar alumni, were delighted when invited to spend an evening with the lively Dr. Hamburg a few years before she passed, as she regaled us with stories about her days at Vassar and at Yale.

Commerce Department friends. *From left:* Pilar Martinez, Lauri, and Marian Pegram; *front left:* Charlotte Kea; and front right: Eileen Cassidy Rivera

I share an organic and rewarding friendship with Merianne de Merode, who, like me, was in the Foreign Service at the US Information Agency though we entered and left at different times. She is the most resilient person I know, thriving beyond what the average person would find insurmountable for the body and soul. She convened a diverse group of her female friends to discuss issues around race and gender after the 2016 election. I doubt we realized then how prescient our group was to begin the conversations that so many now are struggling to initiate. Our personal narratives surface as we tackle difficult topics digesting and respecting the confidentiality and views of each member. We have developed a bond that grows stronger each time we come together, bringing us a sense of renewal and a surge of energy and purpose.

I get together several times a year and communicate regularly with a small group of women with whom I worked for many years and who have become irreplaceable friends. That core group includes my former assistant, Pilar Martinez, several others who started as special assistants along the way—Eileen Cassidy-Rivera, Charlotte Kea—and Marian Pegram who joined us at Commerce. Some were with me in my early days at Gray and Company and at Hill and Knowlton and continued with me to Commerce and even to Iridium. I have mentored them professionally and personally and have gotten to know their families and they mine. Our shared experiences and trust have bound us.

I keep in touch with friends from the Commerce Department and the Clinton administration. While we may have been little more than colleagues then, our relationships deepened, united by the ghosts of our friends lost in the plane crash on St. John's Mountain in 1996. Many of us remain committed to the Ron Brown Scholars, so ably led by Michael Mallory and Vanessa Evans for over twenty years, an incredible family expanded yearly by students selected from a large pool of highly qualified candidates from resilient communities who receive financial support for their college education. The support system extends beyond money to a lifetime of mentoring, guidance, friendship, and emotional support.

Searching for an opportunity to meet with friends and to discuss politics, I formed the Dinner and Discussion Group (DDG). I purposely invited a diverse array of participants from varied racial and ethnic backgrounds, from both party affiliations, from a variety of professions, and across different generations—Jude Kearney, Aaron Williams, Judith Barnett, Debra Carter, Natwar Gandhi, Mark Chichester, Ann Alonzo, Michael Reed, Randa Fahmy Hudome, Peter Romero, and Jill Schuker. We limit ourselves to one conversation and one topic at a time. The collective wisdom of the group has led us to critical discussions and raucous debate, but always ends with enthusiasm for our next reunion.

Nonprofit board service always has been a cornerstone of my commitment to "pay it forward." I chaired for two and served for ten years on the board of the National Education Association Foundation (NEAF) under the able leadership of president and CEO Harriet Sanford, who has become a valued friend. A former colleague and friend from Gray and Company, Bob Witeck, introduced

From left: Janice, Harriet Sanford, Mark Chichester, Robert Adams, Elizabeth Oliver Farrow, and Lauri, Rio de Janeiro

me to the NEAF when Harriet's predecessor Judith Renyi was ending her tenure. I take pride in having contributed to enhanced community engagement programs for teachers and students. Throughout her teaching career, my mother had been a proud member of the NEA.

I am a former vice chair of the nonprofit Global Communities, introduced to me by a friend, David Sloan, and headed by David Weiss. The organization designs and delivers programs focused on housing, education, financing, and builds and strengthens communities throughout the world. The board of trustees was a pleasure to work with. I developed friendships with those on the board and some of their families. I was particularly proud of our work in the Middle East supporting communities subject to the vicissitudes of the region.

I attribute my positive experience with these organizations to their leadership, practical approach, commitment to mission, full engagement of trustees, good governance, and measurable results. Shared expectations and worldviews enhanced my experience and made friendships with board colleagues easy and lasting.

I value tremendously the professional, and intellectual value of programs at the Council on Foreign Relations, where I have been a member since the 1980s.

I am on the Executive Committee of the Association for Diplomatic Studies and Training (ADST). The nonprofit produces oral histories of diplomats and related individuals in the field of foreign affairs, and gives voice to compelling information and materials that increase public understanding and education, encouraging the expansion of diverse, multidimensional records of important international events. The accounts are used for research and education of students, available electronically and at the Library of Congress.

Organizations focused on women, their development, accomplishments, leadership, mentorship, and support are close to my heart. They include Black Girls Magic (BGM), Vital Voices, and the Women's Foreign Policy Group.

The International Women's Forum (IWF) champions women's leadership worldwide under the leadership of president and CEO Stephanie Mathews O'Keefe. The IWF trustees and over 7000 members are representative of the most experienced, accomplished and capable women in the world. A longtime member, I admire the leadership and professional support programs they sponsor. I have been a mentor for women in the Fellows Program, focused on leadership, and the Women Athletes Business Network (WABN). Both programs are highly competitive; the Fellows have sessions at Harvard University and at SINEAD in France; the WABN participants are counseled about transitions from sports careers to other professions. I attended an executive leadership course sponsored by IWF and George Washington University, "On the Board," designed for board ready women to develop relationships and enrich knowledge about serving on boards. Among our international cohort, I made lasting friendships, especially with Penny McIntyre, Sandy Stash and the late Gail McKee. I have received invaluable advice and support from many members in the US and around the globe. We can always be assured that a member will respond to a request from another, much like I imagine sisters in a sorority. Our conferences take place in cities around the world. I have ventured into ballet classes in world capitals with Miami member extraordinaire Toni Randolph's daughter, Tasha Norman, Executive Director, Young Professionals Network and Director of Market Development for ALM Global Newsroom, owner of life-span Pilates and founder of NYC Dance Week.

I am grateful for my many instructors over the years from Vassar College days, Sherrie Dvoretsky, and Jeanne Periolat Czula. My college friend Shanuah Beamon and I rocked a jazz class weekly at DC. Dance Works taught by the late David Holmes in the 1980s. More than a decade ago I returned to regular adult ballet classes primarily with the stellar instructor and coach Aaron Jackson. I have been inspired by the classes and the artistry of Stuart Loungway and the many ballet instructors around the world who have welcomed me into their studios during my travels.

Deep and significant friendships have emerged at crucial junctures in my life for which I am thankful: Steve Sims, passionate advocate for minority business, and who provided crucial advice and support when I was a recent college graduate debating my path forward. New York native Nick Williams, who was among our few Black Foreign Service Officers, assigned to the US Consulate in Guadalajara, Mexico, while I was at the US Embassy in Mexico City. He provided comfort and excitement as we acclimated to our respective homes in Mexico and connection to the lives we left on the other side of the border. Lon Walls, a talented public relations executive, accomplished competitor in the Burmese martial art of Bando, who welcomed me warmly when he was president of the Capital Press Club, and I was new to the profession; and Marcos Koren, a Brazilian diplomat who during his two years here explored the far reaches of my country, visiting sites and studying our history. We lived one floor from each other and conveniently spent hours on our balconies sharing stories about our experiences, politics, and perspectives. This list is far from exhaustive. Those unnamed are not diminished in my thoughts or in my heart.

According to my generous and insightful agent Faith Childs, writing a memoir for some is a difficult and painful journey and for others, pleasurable. It has been a timely and gratifying adventure. I cannot express enough my gratitude to her for finding merit in my work early in the process; guiding and encouraging me through the writing process; and her conviction that my story was important to be shared. I have revisited the past with a seasoned perspective and desire to reexamine previous assumptions. The solitude of the COVID-19 period created the space to think and write. I am grateful for this experience which has opened dialogue with family and friends about things previously unspoken.

I am grateful to my publisher Emily Barrosse, founder of aptly named Bold Story Press (BSP) focusing on women writers, and BSP's team of attentive experts in the industry: Karen Gulliver, Laurie Entringer, and Julianna Scott Fein.

I would like to thank those who have inspired and supported me throughout writing and publishing *Dancing in the Dash*: my family, Joyce M. Fitz, Norman A Fitz, Briana Pegado, Fernando Silverio Pinto Pegado, Fernando Oliveira Pegado, Ana Lwena Sebastiao, Connie Scott and the Mayes family; and the Fitz, Fitts, and Hawkins families.

I am extremely grateful for the inspiration, support, and contributions the following people have made to the development of this book: The Collective, the International Career Advancement (ICAP) family, my "five friends," Erin Bagshaw, Karen Cox, Merianne de Merode and the Beautiful Women sisterhood, Gina Abercrombie-Winstanley, Cecile Ablack, Robert Adams, Pam Anderson, Della Britton Baeza, Judith Barnett, Karen Brown, Steve Chameides, Mark Chichester, Makeba Clay, Ruth Davis, Yvonne De Vastey, Jean-Robert Estimé, Ellena Friedman, Sharon Freeman, Ed Jones, Virginia Johnson, Jim Hackney, Julie Kent, Jennifer Jones, Susan Johnson, Jeroen Koolhaas, Bob Kroll, Donald Lipscomb, Paula Williams Madison, Alia Malek, Denia Massetti, Maria Olsen, LaFleur Paysour, Robert Raben, Saafir Rabb, Ruth Reynolds, Susan Rice, Harriet Sanford, Carolyn Shanoff, Jill Schuker, Paula Stern, Sandra Taylor, Margery Thompson, Reid Weingarten, Aaron Williams, Peter Woicke, Audrey Wolf, and Miomir Zuzul.

You have all been my corps de ballet on this journey. To you, "Reverence."

Lauri, Palacio de Avellaneda, Peñaranda de Duero, Spain, *photographer Santiago Martinez*

Index

Bold Story Press is a curated, woman-owned hybrid publishing company with a mission of publishing well-written stories by women. If your book is chosen for publication, our team of expert editors and designers will work with you to publish a professionally edited and designed book. Every woman has a story to tell. If you have written yours and want to explore publishing with Bold Story Press, contact us at https://boldstorypress.com.

BOLD STORY PRESS

The Bold Story Press logo, designed by Grace Arsenault, was inspired by the nom de plume, or pen name, a sad necessity at one time for female authors who wanted to publish. The woman's face hidden in the quill is the profile of Virginia Woolf, who, in addition to being an early feminist writer, founded and ran her own publishing company, Hogarth Press.

CPSIA information can be obtained
at www.ICGtesting.com
Printed in the USA
LVHW111929210822
726495LV00004B/448